PERSPECTIVES ON SOUTHERN AFRICA

*Education, Race, and Social Change
in South Africa*

Members of the USSALEP Team

Vera K. Farris
Vice-President for Academic Affairs
Kean College

Richard C. Gilman
President, Occidental College

Lawrence J. Keller
Director, Independent Study Program
Indiana University

John A. Marcum
Academic Vice-Chancellor
University of California, Santa Cruz

Walter E. Massey
Director, Argonne National Laboratory
University of Chicago

Marvin Wachman
President, Temple University

Education, Race, and Social Change in South Africa

John A. Marcum

*For the Study Team
of the United States–South Africa
Leader Exchange Program*

UNIVERSITY OF CALIFORNIA PRESS
BERKELEY   LOS ANGELES   LONDON

University of California Press
Berkeley and Los Angeles, California

University of California Press, Ltd.
London, England

© 1982 by
The Regents of the University of California

Library of Congress Cataloging in Publication Data
Main entry under title:

Education, race, and social change in South Africa.
  (Perspectives on Southern Africa; 34)
  Includes bibliographical references and index.
  1. Education—South Africa.   2. Blacks—Education—
South Africa.   3. South Africa—Race relations.
I. Marcum, John A.   II. United States-South Africa
Leader Exchange Program. Study Team.   III. Series.
LA1536.E36   1982   370'.968   82-60256
IBSN 0-520-04855-5
ISBN 0-520-04899-7 (pbk.)

Printed in the United States of America

1 2 3 4 5 6 7 8 9

For Arthur

Contents

Preface

IT SEEMED A propitious time for a group of American educators to explore first-hand the changing circumstances and prospects of South African higher education. A national study commission in South Africa had just completed a major review of the country's educational system and needs. Manpower shortages were forcing relaxation of the color bar in some skilled jobs and professions. And state expenditures for black education were increasing amidst sharp debate about the direction in which it should develop. Thus it was that in early 1981, the United States–South Africa Leader Exchange Program (USSALEP) decided to sponsor a visit by a team of senior American university administrators to South Africa.

Founded in 1958, USSALEP is a private, multiracial association of Americans and South Africans of diverse backgrounds committed to "the fostering of open and direct human links among all people by whom the history of South Africa will be shaped." Its programs include mid-career development projects to facilitate the entry of blacks into management and leadership positions within South Africa, and symposia and team visits that reach across group divisions to break down stereotypes and promote authentic communication. In the words of former Executive Director Helen Kitchen, "USSALEP sees its primary role as that of a catalyst—quietly fostering the creative interaction of individuals and organizations."

USSALEP sent an initial group of American educators to South Africa in July 1978. Made up of college and university presidents, it was led by Reverend Theodore Hesburgh of Notre Dame and included Elias Blake (Clark College), Robert Good (Denison University), Robben Fleming (University of Michigan), and Adele Simmons (Hampshire College). The team surveyed educational and social issues and released an end-of-visit statement that decried South Africa's racial segregation and political repression. It called for "massive" change toward "meaningful political participation for all South Africans" and predicted that without this change, "opportunities for nonviolent solutions" to the country's problems would be "forfeited." American relations with South African universities, it concluded, would suffer so long as American scholars were "arbitrarily" denied visas and so long as "freedom of speech and assembly [were] imperiled and faculty and students alike [were obliged to] pursue their studies in an environment in which they [could] be banned or detained." The Hesburgh team urged the South African government to abandon apartheid and embark upon discussion with all racial groups with an eye to creating a new political order within which all universities would be racially open and there would be a single, unified ministry of education.

The second USSALEP university team visited South Africa in August–September 1981. It concentrated its inquiry on the character, quality, and accessibility of South African higher education. Representing a wide spectrum of American institutions, this second, multiracial team led by John A. Marcum, Academic Vice-Chancellor of the University of California at Santa Cruz, included Vera K. Farris, Vice-President for Academic Affairs, Kean College; Lawrence J. Keller, Director of the Independent Study Program, Indiana University; Richard C. Gilman, President of Occidental College; Walter E. Massey,

Director of the Argonne National Laboratory, University of Chicago; and Marvin Wachman, President of Temple University. The team travelled extensively; met with faculty, students, administrators, and trustees of some fifteen universities and technikons; and consulted a wide range of education, business, press, government, and community leaders. Assisted by a grant from Nedbank of South Africa and the staff of USSALEP's Pretoria office headed by Willem I. Grobler, the team met everywhere with frankness, courtesy, and cooperation.

Persuaded of the significance of educational issues and change, and of the importance of what they had learned, the team deliberated at length on how Americans might most effectively contribute to expanding the quality and outreach of education for black South Africans. The team presented and discussed its preliminary policy recommendations at a December 17, 1981 conference on "Furthering Higher Education of Black South Africans: How Can the United States Best Help?" organized by the African Studies Program of Georgetown University's Center for Strategic and International Studies (CSIS). Profiting from this exchange with others concerned with South Africa's educational needs and challenges, including members of a study mission of the U.S. Agency for International Development (AID) who had just returned from South Africa, the team held its final deliberations. A grant from the Carnegie Corporation to USSALEP in support of this book's publication is enabling the team to share the results of its mission with a wide audience.

The Introduction and Findings, written by Dr. Marcum, are followed by an extensive selection of documents. With the exception of the address by Assistant Secretary of State Chester A. Crocker that concludes the section, the documents were culled from a mass of materials gathered by the team on its visit and concern South Africa's educational present and future.

The author and entire team are enormously grateful for the generosity and openness with which South Africans from all communities assisted this undertaking. Though it is not possible to cite all who deserve acknowledgement, the following persons must be mentioned as having contributed importantly to the success of the project: Helen Kitchen, her successor as Executive Director, Steven McDonald, and the staff of USSALEP's headquarters in Washington, D.C., for administrative support; Dawid de Villiers, Managing Director of Nasionale Pers Beperk and Chairman of USSALEP's Management Committee, for facilitating the visit in South Africa; Peter Vale (South African Institute of International Affairs) and Mary McMahon (University of California at Santa Cruz) for research assistance; the following Rectors, Principals, or Directors who facilitated exchanges with faculty and students at their institutions: J. P. de Lange (Rand Afrikaans University); D. J. du Plessis (University of Witwatersrand); D. M. Joubert (University of Pretoria); P. C. Mokgokong (University of the North); Theo van Wijk (University of South Africa); Stuart J. Saunders (University of Cape Town); Mike J. de Vries (University of Stellenbosch); Richard van der Ross (University of Western Cape); Franklin Sonn (Peninsula Technikon); S. P. Olivier (University of Durban-Westville); A. C. Nkabinde (University of Zululand); N. D. Clarence (University of Natal); A. M. Setsabi (National University of Lesotho); and B. de van der Merwe (University of Transkei). Others who made special contributions to the study include: Kenneth B. Hartshorne (Chairman, Council of the University of Bophuthatswana); Professor Es'kia Mphahlele (University of Witwatersrand); Hennie Reynders (Chairman, National Manpower Commission); Jaap Strydom (Regional Director, Department of Education and Training, Johannesburg); Bishop Desmond Tutu (Chair, Educational Opportunities Council); John Saul (Director, South African Educational Trust—SACHED); John C. Rees (Director, South African Institute of Race Relations); Gerrit Viljoen (Minister of National Education); Chief Gatsha Buthelezi (Chief Minister, KwaZulu); Hans Hallen and Pat Poovalingham (community leaders in Durban); Jannie de Villiers (past Rector, University of Stellenbosch); Professor Walton R. Johnson (Rutgers University); and Raymond Smyke (Assistant Secretary, World Confederation of Organizations of the Teaching Profession, Geneva).

Introduction

I

The origins of higher education in South Africa date back more than 150 years. In 1829 the Cape Colony established a South African College to prepare students for advanced study abroad. Precursor to the present-day University of Cape Town, the College subsequently began offering post-secondary courses of its own. In the 1870s the University of Cape of Good Hope was created as an examining body to serve South African College and other emergent institutions, notably St. Andrew's College (1855), now Rhodes University, and Stellenbossche Gymnasium (1866), now the University of Stellenbosch. Similar to colonial colleges founded in other British overseas settlements, these schools were patterned after English "redbrick" and Scottish institutions of higher education. Their students were almost exclusively white. Their faculties came from Britain and Europe.

Creation of the Union of South Africa (1910) in the wake of the Boer War opened a new era in South African education and politics. A series of University Acts in 1916 reorganized higher education throughout the Union. These acts founded the South African

Native College (University of Fort Hare) for blacks,[1] formed the Joint Matriculation Board to set University entrance requirements, and established the University of South Africa (UNISA) as a nationwide, post-secondary examining body.

Under the self-governing Union, which merged the former Boer republics of Transvaal and the Orange Free State with Britain's Cape Colony and Natal, higher education mirrored the cultural and linguistic duality of South Africa's white population. Afrikaans-medium universities—Stellenbosch, Pofchefstroom, Pretoria, and Orange Free State—developed as centers of Afrikaner cultural consciousness and learning. Relatively autonomous institutions, they adopted strict policies against the admission of blacks and drew their faculty and staff largely from South Africa's Afrikaner community.

English-medium universities—Cape Town, Witwatersrand, Rhodes, Natal—modeled themselves on British academic traditions, drew on British faculty, and refrained from imposing a direct color bar. Though enrollment was open, residential, social, and athletic facilities were not. Few blacks were able to qualify for admission. Few were able to finance university studies. Consequently, as late as 1957, black students (Africans, Coloureds, Indians) comprised no more than 5 to 6 percent of the student body at the country's two principal open universities, Cape Town and Witwatersrand. Instead, it was the small (489 students by 1959), English-medium, black but ethnically diverse University College of Fort Hare that developed as the intellectual center of black higher education.

Bilingual (English-Afrikaans) university education did not develop as a unifying force within white society. During the interwar period of 1920–1940, Afrikaans-medium universities expanded and achieved more comprehensive curricula. They quickly drew Afrikaner students away from English-language institutions.

1. Unless the context requires differentiation among Coloureds, Africans, Indians, and (other) Asians, the term "black" will be used to refer without distinction to all persons not generally categorized as white. Under South African law, "African" is a racial classification referring to any person "who is, or is generally accepted as, a member of any aboriginal race or tribe of Africa." The term "Coloured" denotes South Africans of mixed race, generally Afrikaans-speaking and of Afro-European descent.

During this same period, the University of South Africa (UNISA) emerged as the country's one linguistically and communally inclusive institution of higher education. In the 1940s it began offering correspondence courses in English and Afrikaans that were open to South Africans of all racial backgrounds. Later, in 1964, there was an effort to create a bilingual residential university within the white community. The University of Port Elizabeth, however, developed as a predominantly Afrikaans-medium university.[2]

With the electoral triumph of the National party and the rise of Afrikaners to political dominance in 1948, South African universities, along with most other social and political institutions of the country, entered a new era of change. The Union of South Africa became the Republic of South Africa and left the British Commonwealth. Afrikaans-medium universities prospered and expanded, benefiting from new funding for their facilities, staff, and research. The National party government pressed a strict segregationist doctrine upon higher education. In 1953 it created a special commission to "investigate and report on the practicability and financial implications of providing separate training facilities for non-Europeans at universities."[3] The all-white commission concluded that if separate universities were established for them, there would be no objection on the part of blacks.[4] After lengthy debate within the government about how best to achieve this end, parliament passed the Extension of the University Education Act of 1959. That act created new state-administered universities for

2. The desire of political conservatives to establish a regional, Eastern Cape alternative to the relatively liberal (English-medium) Rhodes University at Grahamstown may have been a motive more central to the creation of the University of Port Elizabeth than the unrealized goal of bilingualism. See David Welsh, "Some Political and Social Determinants of the Academic Environment," in Hendrick W. van der Merwe and David Welsh, eds., *Student Perspectives on South Africa* (Cape Town: David Philip, 1972), pp. 27-29.

For a succinct overview of the history of higher education in South Africa see David J. Crammer and Valerie A. Woolston, *Southern Africa*, World Education Series (Washington, D.C.: American Association of Collegiate Registrars and Admissions Officers, 1980), pp. 1–8.

3. RSA, *Government Notice No. 2789*, December 18, 1953.

4. See A. L. Behr, *New Perspectives in South African Education* (Durban: Butterworths, 1978), p. 136.

Africans, Coloureds, and Indians and denied to all universities the right to admit students from outside their ascribed racial group without special government permission. The law established separate universities for (1) Sotho, Tsonga, and Venda speakers (University of the North at Turfloop, Transvaal); (2) Zulu and Swazi speakers (University of Zululand at Empangeni, Natal); (3) Xhosa speakers (Fort Hare University, Alice [Ciskei], Eastern Cape); (4) Coloureds (University of Western Cape, Bellville, Cape Town); and (5) Indians (University of Durban-Westville, Natal). These ethnic universities, the first three of which are physically remote and all of which are isolated from the mainstream of white South African intellectual life, are directly funded by the government and are administered under the direction of either the Department of Education and Training (formerly Bantu Education) or Department of Internal Affairs (for Coloureds and Indians). As of 1980, the faculties remained predominantly white (mostly Afrikaners): 441 lecturers out of 621 at the African universities, 185 out of 247 at Western Cape, 224 out of 346 at Durban-Westville.[5] A separate Department of National Education oversees South Africa's state-subsidized but comparatively more autonomous white universities.

University enrollment reflects the duality of South African society. In 1974, white enrollment in tertiary (university and advanced technical) education totalled 95,589, or 2.3 percent of the white population, a percentage approaching the overall U.S. figure of 3.26 percent. That same year, African enrollment totalled 7,845, or .04 percent of the African population, a figure midway between Ghana's .06 percent and Tanzania's .02 percent. The overall enrollment figure for South Africa was 110,808 tertiary level students, or .45 percent of the population, well below the percentage in such developed industrial states as Japan (1.61 percent) and West Germany (1.03 percent), but closer to that of an industrializing state such as Spain (.87 percent). In 1976, enrollment in tertiary education constituted the following percentages of South Africa's four official racial communities: Africans, .06;

5. *Survey of Race Relations in South Africa, 1980* (Johannesburg: South African Institute of Race Relations, 1981), p. 538.

TABLE 1
Student Enrollment in South African Universities

		English-language Universities	Afrikaans-language Universities	Ethnic Universities	Subtotal	% of Subtotal	Correspondence (UNISA)	Total	% of Total
1954	W	10,736	8,915	0	19,651	94.2	3,305	22,956	91.4
	C	221	0	36	257	1.3	131	388	1.6
	A/I	414	0	19	433	2.0	282	715	3.0
	Af	200	0	314	514	2.5	555	1,069	4.0
1958	W	ˋ12,019	12,218	0	24,237	93.8	5,538	29,775	89.6
	C	350	0	48	398	1.5	209	607	1.8
	A/I	606	0	47	653	2.5	565	1,218	3.7
	Af	269	0	283	552	2.2	1,085	1,637	4.9
1965	W	17,006	21,651	0	38,657	91.8	12,078	50,735	89.3
	C	297	0	418	715	1.7	427	1,142	2.0
	A/I	647	0	1,009	1,656	3.9	875	2,531	4.5
	Af	147	0	956	1,103	2.6	1,310	2,413	4.2
1971	W	24,701	32,281	0	56,982	89.8	20,239	77,221	86.9
	C	359	0	934	1,293	2.0	739	2,032	2.3
	A/I	857	0	1,710	2,567	4.1	1,662	4,229	4.8
	Af	224	0	2,379	2,603	4.1	2,804	5,407	6.0
1974	W	27,801	40,807	0	68,608	88.4	26,981	95,589	85.5
	C	523	2	1,440	1,965	2.5	1,177	3,142	2.8
	A/I	884	0	2,342	3,226	4.1	2,006	5,232	4.7
	Af	305	4	3,541	3,850	5.0	3,995	7,845	7.0
1978	W	30,045	50,237	41	80,323	84.0	38,257	118,580	80.1
	C	884	30	2,975	3,889	4.0	2,420	6,309	4.3
	A/I	1,368	23	4,312	5,703	6.0	3,927	9,630	6.5
	Af	482	19	5,164	5,665	6.0	7,796	13,461	9.1
1980	W	31,479	51,256	151	82,886	80.7	37,404	120,290	75.7
	C	1,247	129	4,005	5,381	5.2	2,822	8,203	5.1
	A/I	1,858	47	4,908	6,813	6.6	5,261	12,074	7.6
	Af	734	54	6,954	7,742	7.5	10,687	18,429	11.6

W = white; C = Coloured; A/I = Asian/Indian; Af = African

SOURCE: Table 1 and Figs. 1 and 2 based on data from the South African Institute of Race Relations' annual *Survey of Race Relations in South Africa*.

NOTE: Figures for Transkei included as available; Medunsa (new black medical school) not included. University of Port Elizabeth enrollment included as Afrikaans-language.

Coloureds, .13; Asians, .75; whites, 2.52; overall, .51.[6] That year, 11,314 whites and 563 Africans obtained university degrees.

Enrollment trends over the past quarter-century are shown in Table 1 (page 5) and Figs. 1 and 2 (pages 7 and 8). They confirm the ascent of Afrikaans-medium universities and a long lag in the development of black, especially African, higher education.

II

The full meaning of such quantitative data can be appreciated only when accompanied by a searching inquiry into the qualitative dimensions of education. Accordingly, the USSALEP team needed to gain a fuller understanding of the social context and dynamics of South African higher education and to learn of trends and problems in primary and secondary education that constrain or foster quantitative and qualitative development of higher education. What, for example, are the prospects for universal primary education? Can qualified teachers be trained and facilities be constructed to achieve that goal in the next decade? Is there a calendared plan for doing so? Can the South African economy support the effort? With a population base comparable to that of South Africa, California spends annually $12 billion on kindergarten through twelfth grade (K–12) and $3 billion on higher education. What transformation of the South African economy would be required to attain such educational funding levels?

Is South African higher education providing the quantity and quality of scientific and technological education that will enable the country to expand its modern economic sector to include all communities? How many South Africans go abroad for advanced study in scientific and technological fields? Are enrollments in economy-related fields such as computer and

6. Statistics derived from the UNESCO *Statistical Yearbook* and the South African Institute of Race Relations' annual *Survey of Race Relations in South Africa*. See F. M. Orkin, L. O. Nicholaysen, Max Price, "The Future of the Urban University in South Africa: Some Practical Considerations," *Social Dynamics* 5, no. 1 (Cape Town: 1979), p. 30.

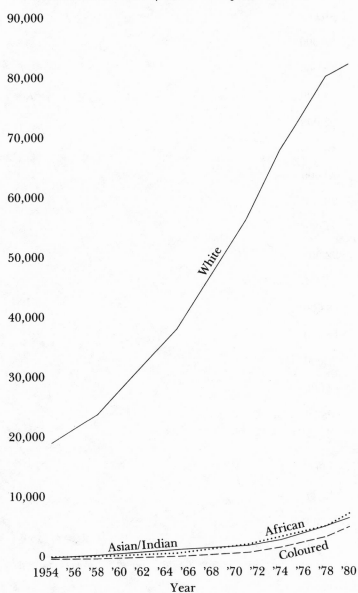

FIGURE 1
South African Universities (Residential)
Student Enrollment by Racial Group (1954–1980)

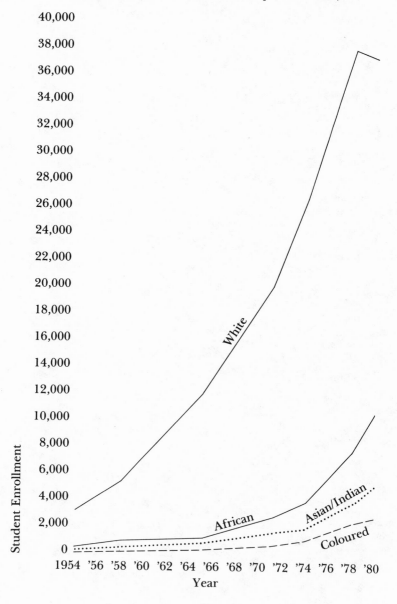

FIGURE 2
University of South Africa (Correspondence)
Student Enrollment by Racial Group (1954–1980)

information science, geology, agriculture, and business management expanding importantly—and, if so, for blacks as well as for whites?

Quality and creativity in higher education require not only financial and human resources but also a climate of academic freedom. What is the status of academic freedom in South African universities? What is the role of faculties in the governance of their institutions? Have university faculties been socialized into American or European concepts of academic freedom? How do resources for research and library holdings compare with those of American universities? What constraints are placed upon research, scientific or social? Is instruction or research handicapped by policies restricting access to publications?

What is the extent of inter-university collaboration, between or among English- and Afrikaans-medium institutions, between white and black universities? Conversely, to what extent are South African universities isolated from one another and from their communities? Are there active, nationwide, interracial professional associations for intellectual disciplines such as chemistry, psychology, and literature?

Nearly a third of South Africans pursuing higher education do so through correspondence courses with UNISA. What is the quality of such education and what is its potential for outreach into communities not heretofore able to enroll for advanced schooling? Do South Africans enroll in foreign correspondence courses?

It is now widely acknowledged in South Africa not only that higher education is vital to the social and economic development of all communities but that there is need for a massive expansion of black education. The once open universities of Witwatersrand and Cape Town and now even such closed universities as Stellenbosch have begun to open their doors to black students in significant numbers. Will this trend continue, broaden? What problems and potentials does it create? What does it augur for the future of ethnic universities?

What is the quality of education at the ethnic universities founded since 1959? Of particular concern are the background and quality of faculty, extent of academic freedom, breadth and appropriateness of curricula, adequacy of financial support, status of library and research facilities, and geographical accessibility.

From these many questions arises one that is overriding. Is there an emerging vision and set of national priorities to guide the development of South African higher education? Or will parochial values continue to shape, restrict, and segment it and other levels of South African education?

III

The centrality of education to South Africa's future has been stressed repeatedly by South African economic leaders. Notable is Anglo-American chairman Harry F. Oppenheimer. In a statement to his corporation in 1981, he affirmed his view that "the gap between black education and white remains the most serious obstacle to economic growth and better race relations in South Africa. The government has pledged itself to provide equal education and training for all race groups but the rate of advance is painfully slow and gross inequities persist."[7]

Oppenheimer illustrated some of the factors obstructing progress: an estimated teacher-pupil ratio of 1 to 46[8] in African schools as compared to 1 to 19 in white schools; the fact that only 16 percent of nearly 73,000 African teachers have attained the educational level required of white teachers; racial prejudice that has resulted in "a surplus of places in well-equipped technical colleges and technikons[9] for whites at a time when there is a critical shortage of such facilities for blacks." Oppenheimer

7. "Statement by the Chairman Mr. H. F. Oppenheimer" (Delivered to Anglo-American Corporation of South Africa Ltd., Johannesburg, June 30, 1981).

8. Other estimates run as high as 1 to 56. See E. G. Malherbe, "Conflict and Progress in Education," in Ellen Hellmann and Henry Lever, eds., *Conflict and Progress: Fifty Years of Race Relations in South Africa* (Johannesburg: Macmillan South Africa, 1979), p. 171.

9. Technikons are tertiary, polytechnic institutions that provide training in technological, scientific, and related skills.

argues that the expense of building and staffing separate, less adequate facilities for blacks compounds the problems of unequal training and shortage of qualified teachers. To achieve proper educational goals, he states, the government must adopt "an altogether more urgent, bolder approach." This injunction gives rise to the question of whether the concepts of affirmative action and compensatory education have been considered for part of such an approach.

Are there ways in which Americans or American experience might contribute to an educational breakthrough in South Africa? In the light of the team's inquiry into the character, quality, accessibility, and needs of South African higher education, how might American higher education most appropriately respond? Are there activities that might be undertaken within South Africa that would not entail a compromising support of racial separation, e.g. activities focused on faculty exchange, books and instructional materials, study by correspondence? Might support of higher education in neighboring states such as Lesotho and Zimbabwe offer a comparatively economical means of providing educational opportunity for South Africans outside the apartheid system? Do scholarship/study opportunities (e.g. the Institute of International Education [IIE] program) in the United States and Europe offer the optimum means for providing rigorous, quality education to a select number of South African blacks? What, if any, combination of these various approaches might seem appropriate?

To refine, augment, and seek answers to such questions was the central charge of the USSALEP university team.

Findings of the USSALEP Team

EDUCATIONAL DEVELOPMENT is arguably the strongest force for social change in South Africa. An acute shortage of skilled manpower in an expanding economy is obliging the government to open the doors of educational opportunity to aspiring blacks. The pace and extent of this change, as well as its character and aims, remain matters of sharp public and private disagreement. Thus the USSALEP university team witnessed fervent national debate over educational issues central to its own inquiry.

Discussions with educational and civic leaders on and off South African university campuses enabled the team to study the scope and nature of educational change and to consider ways Americans might constructively respond to it. Though constrained by time, the team surveyed higher education in sufficient depth to arrive at answers, albeit incomplete or tentative, to the questions providing the impetus for its mission. It found that South Africa does *not* yet have a single, emergent vision or a set of national priorities to guide the development of education. Indeed, the team found that the separate institutions, discriminatory policies, and communal inequalities that had prompted an earlier (1978) USSALEP team of American university presidents to urge comprehensive reform remained tenaciously in place.[1]

But the team also observed promising ferment at two levels. First, a series of educational policy studies and conferences culminating in a massive government-funded research effort carried out under the auspices of the Human Sciences Research Council (HSRC) had amassed data, focused discussion, and given rise to expectations of new, coherent governmental initiatives. Second, economic and demographic pressures had induced a rise in black enrollments at all levels of education and fostered different groups' opposing sets of hopes and anxieties regarding the quality of black education and the possible long-term sociopolitical consequences of its expansion.

The USSALEP team found that South Africa clearly needs more people who can provide the right answers to complex technical questions—and more people who can formulate the right questions about enduring social, economic, and political imbalances and conflicts. South Africa needs an educational system that will go beyond traditional rote learning to enhance its citizenry's capacity to criticize, analyze, and create—its capacity, in other words, to solve problems.

The Dynamics of Educational Change

Few observers in or out of South Africa foresee near-term political reform of the kind likely to produce truly comprehensive educational reform. South African academics seem generally to share the view of the UNISA political scientist Willem Kleynhans that current trends in Afrikaner politics do not favor major near-term constitutional change.[2] And despite political aliena-

1. At the close of its visit on July 22, the 1978 team issued a statement in Johannesburg calling for a prompt end to racial segregation in higher education and for moves to assure full participation by all South Africans in the governance of their country.

2. Hermann Giliomee, Professor of History at the University of Stellenbosch, identifies three processes of reform that he believes Prime Minister P. W. Botha will pursue: (1) The process of educating and training blacks, allowing them upward economic mobility into a middle class status that will

tion and latent revolutionary sentiment reflected, for example, in opinion surveys and conversations with black students, black political dissent is strictly circumscribed.[3]

In labor and education, however, reformist activism is acquiring considerable punch. The 1979 decision of the Nationalist government to grant limited trade union rights to blacks has resulted in a rapid growth of registered and unregistered labor organizations. Empowered to raise money, negotiate, and strike, unions have now organized approximately 5 percent of the black work force. Reinforced by a parallel growth in black consumer power, they have begun to test the weapons of collective bargaining. Concomitantly, professional training for black South African labor leaders ranks with financial help for Poland's independent labor movement, Solidarity, as a priority of AFL-CIO and other international labor assistance. The South African government, however, has responded to perceived signs of community-linked militancy or political radicalism

---

give them a "vested interest in political stability and capitalism;" (2) The process of "regional development aimed at alleviating the poverty of the homelands, which will hopefully lead to a decentralization of power to the regions where mechanisms of consultation between the races would be built from the ground up;" (3) "The process of granting political representation to Coloured people and Indians and erecting the organizational structures of a confederation of states. This would start a process of political consultation, leading to joint decision-making on the national level and ultimately to power sharing. For this the government has created the President's Council, which may be converted into an elected body after the government's constituency has grown accustomed to whites and blacks sitting down to talk about new constitutional arrangements." *Rand Daily Mail*, October 21, 1981.

3. An August 1981 poll of urban blacks by the Johannesburg *Star* showed the African National Congress (ANC) with an overall 40 percent support rating. *Africa News* 17, no. 18 (Durham, N.C.: November 2, 1981). Also in August 1981, the Security Police announced that since January black (principally ANC) dissidents had committed "37 acts of terrorism" against rail, power, police, and military installations. *Citizen* (Johannesburg), August 30, 1981. To date, black violence manifests itself mostly in self-destructive social anomie. During the visit of the USSALEP team, the *Star* (September 7, 1981) reported briefly that on just one weekend twenty-two persons in Soweto were stabbed to death and many others seriously wounded in knife attacks. (By way of comparison, in the large metropole of Paris, the press treated the murders of twelve persons over the full month of July 1981 as a major story. *Journal du Dimanche*, September 13, 1981.)

among labor organizers by jailing top union leadership almost as fast as it is trained. Education, the second arena of significant reform, is also undergoing massive, though confused, change. Beneath the surface of continuing political stalemate powerful forces are at work that will radically recast South African education.

Increasing dependence on skilled black labor is a basic reality of contemporary South Africa. Africans, mostly unskilled, now constitute 70 percent of the total South African workforce.[4] Within the next ten years they are expected to furnish 88 percent of the country's skilled manpower. This means mass education.

In the twenty years between 1980 and 2000 South Africa's African population is expected to grow from 19.5 million to 29 million, that is, to 75 percent of the total population. The white population will only increase from 4.5 to 5 million—down from 16.5 to 13.2 percent of the total.[5] The shrinking proportion of whites will be unable to provide the cadres of high-level professional, technical, and managerial manpower necessary for South Africa to sustain and expand a complex industrial economy. Accordingly, the country's National Manpower Commission has warned that South Africa cannot "realise its development potential and offer all its people an acceptable standard of living if it persists in trying to draw its [high-level manpower] mainly from the White population." Such a policy can only lead to a "relative deterioration in economic conditions."[6]

4. As of 1980, 40 percent of economically active Africans in urban areas had no education and an additional 42 percent had less than five years of school. Corresponding percentages for rural areas were 65 and 29. Source: U.S. Embassy, Pretoria.

5. These and all subsequent statistics include Bophuthatswana, Transkei, and Venda. Projecting out forty years to 2020, demographers of the Human Sciences Research Council foresee the following population: Whites, 5.3 million (11.1 percent); Coloureds, 4 million (8.4 percent); Asians, 1.3 million (2.7 percent); Africans, 36.8 million (77.8 percent)—a total of 47.3 million people. RSA, Department of Manpower Utilization, *Report of the National Manpower Commission for the Period January 1, 1980–December 31, 1980*, Pretoria, January 30, 1981, p. 146.

6. Ibid., p. 51.

Optimistically, government sources predict a doubling of the number of Africans in professional and clerical occupations between 1977 and 1987. However, on the basis of current educational trends, they project relatively little change in the racial composition of the managerial sector. According to the National Manpower Commission, 96 percent of the managerial sector was white in 1978, leaving 81 percent of the population in a "state of economic dependence." By 1987, warns the Commission, whites may still constitute 95.5 percent of those "responsible for decisions and action leading to economic growth and job opportunities." Given that the "multi-cultural" nature of South Africa's population requires even more managerial persons than would be the case for a more homogeneous society, the Commission concludes that priority must be given to the development of relevant black professional and technical education.[7]

Behind this Commission recommendation, of course, lies an ideological premise. It holds that South Africa should pay the considerable manpower costs of managerial and administrative redundancies occasioned by separate development. It does not require a brief for separate development, however, to appreciate the urgent need to prepare more blacks for decision-making roles in the private and public sectors of South African society. An awareness of demography will suffice.

White university enrollments, up from 6,500 to 107,000 between 1927 and 1977, have, in fact, reached a stage of diminishing growth. Some educators, for example, Rector Mike de Vries of Stellenbosch, even argue that the proportion of whites enrolled is too large, causing university standards to suffer. Others opine that excessively high white university enrollment contributes to the high student attrition rate and argue that some students should be redirected to technical schools.[8] That leaves but one large, untapped source of potential student talent—blacks.

The distribution of education among population groups has already changed substantially. In 1927, 53.6 percent of South

7. Ibid., pp. 128–129.
8. E. G. Malherbe, "Conflict and Progress in Education," in Ellen Hellmann and Henry Lever, eds., *Conflict and Progress: Fifty Years of Race Relations in South Africa* (Johannesburg: MacMillan South Africa, 1979), p. 166.

TABLE 1

Expected Numbers of Secondary (high school) Pupils in
South Africa and Namibia (South West Africa) Combined

	Whites	Coloured	Indian	African
1980	430,330	161,659	91,717	966,971
1985	461,327	188,132	100,986	1,423,484
1990	400,071	211,410	98,453	2,302,942
1995	364,064	263,303	94,886	3,451,409
2000	367,318	304,210	99,110	4,704,774
2005	370,712	356,503 ˙	102,746	5,913,974
2010	360,190	396,133	103,472	6,613,000

SOURCE: University of Cape Town, November 1980.

Africa's school population was white; in 1977, the figure was
16.4 percent.[9] In the past twenty-five years, the number of African school-goers increased from one million to 4.7 million.
However, the government's new (1981) policy of progressively
introducing compulsory primary education for blacks is expected, if and when fully implemented by the year 2000, to require annual expenditures of roughly $4 billion and a cadre of
320,000 teachers. This translates into 11,000 new teachers and
10,000 new classrooms per year.[10] The willingness of the white
electorate and government to provide the resources to meet this
demand remains decidedly untested.

Total African secondary school enrollment rose from 35,000
in 1955 to 209,000 in 1974, then leapt to 658,000 in 1979.[11] Un-
fortunately, this growth lowered the quality of secondary education by placing impossible demands on an inadequate, static
teaching force. The number of Africans reaching standard ten

9. Ibid., pp. 160–161.
10. Report of the National Manpower Commission, p. 14.
11. According to G. J. Rousseau, Director General of the Department of
Education and Training, Rand Daily Mail (Extra), June 3, 1981. See also the
comprehensive overview article by former Bantu education official Kenneth
B. Hartshorne, "The Unfinished Business: Education for South Africa's Black
People," Optima 30, no. 1 (July 31, 1981), pp. 16–35.

(twelfth grade) rose significantly (from 2,938 to 31,071) only in the past decade (1970–1980).[12] The number of African secondary school graduates doubled between 1975 and 1978 (from 5,529 to 11,167) and is expected to rise to 186,922 by the year 2000. At that time, African graduates will outnumber whites 3 to 1. Add Coloureds and Indians and the ratio will be 4 to 1.[13]

Speaking in parliament, M.P. Horace van Rensburg of the opposition Progressive Federal Party (PFP) recently cited such predictions as reasons that "white domination" cannot persist. By the year 2000, he said, 4 out of every 5 matriculants will be black, 4 of every 5 skilled workers will be black, 19 out of every 20 unskilled workers will be black, collectively blacks will probably be earning more money and paying more income taxes than whites, and if blacks have not by then attained political rights, "they will use their labour organisations with devastating effect."[14]

That van Rensburg's projections for education and skills may represent more than wishful thinking is suggested by the government's 1981–82 budget. Though constricted by declining gold prices and revenues, it includes sharp increases in two sectors: defense (30 percent) and African education (51 percent). Officials of the Department of Manpower Utilization anticipate that expenditures for education must rise from the current 16 percent to 32 percent of the state budget to meet the educational goals of the next decade. This rise, of course, assumes both a steady political will and a steadily expanding economy.

The government has declared that it intends to provide Africans with education of an "absolutely equal standard" to that of whites.[15] If it is to do so, it will have to overcome great disparities in educational quality. In the 1950s and 1960s, government policy was to develop a distinct and largely pretechnological "Bantu education" system based on vernacular languages and ethnic

12. *Report of the National Manpower Commission*, p. 170.
13. Ibid., pp. 170–171.
14. *Argus* (Cape Town), August 25, 1981.
15. Dr. F. Hartzenberg, Minister of Education and Training (Speech to House of Assembly, Standing Committee 3, May 23, 1980), quoted in *Rand Daily Mail* (Extra), June 3, 1981.

culture. Steady deterioration in the quality of African education was the result. The system has been modified in recent years, but the government still insists that through their first four years of schooling, African students must be taught totally in a vernacular. This requirement continues to impede students' proficiency in English, knowledge of which is widely held by Africans to constitute an indispensable window on the world.

The inferior quality of English instruction in black schools constitutes a related handicap. The separation of English and Afrikaans schools by the Nationalists after 1948 lowered the level of bilingualism in all schools. In particular, the English-language competence of Afrikaner teachers suffered. Since 70 percent of teachers came to be drawn from Afrikaans-medium institutions, their lowered proficiency was in turn inflicted upon African students. Afrikaner teachers naturally preferred teaching in Afrikaans. But in 1976, Soweto students rioted and ultimately gained exemption from imposed instruction in Afrikaans.

Given general African resistance to education in either Bantu or Afrikaans vernaculars,[16] the need to improve the standards of English language instruction forms an urgent part of a still larger task, that of raising the qualifications of thousands of African and Coloured teachers. It is these teachers who must assume the principal responsibility for black educational development. The full extent of their handicap is shown in Table 2.

The poorly trained, insecure secondary teacher is fated to "survival teaching." Faced with a generation of young people that is "increasingly socially and politically aware, exposed to the influence of mass media, and questioning of established norms and values," he tries to avoid discussion and discourages questions. He seeks security in the textbook and in traditional didactic teaching methods. He shies away from new ideas and

---

16. It was only in 1925 that Afrikaans displaced High Dutch to become with English an officially sanctioned language of instruction. Afrikaners seem to project the intensity of their own struggle against the linguistic imperialism of English upon Africans whom they believe do, or ought to, feel a similar sense of ethno-linguistic nationalism.

TABLE 2
Qualifications of Teachers (1977)

	White	Indian	Coloured	African
Percentage with university degree	29.6	18.2	3.7	2.2
Percentage with at least matric (secondary education)	64.9	63.9	24.0	12.1
TOTALS	94.5	82.1	27.7	14.3

SOURCE: E. G. Malherbe, "Conflict and Progress in Education," in Ellen Hell-mann and Henry Lever, eds., *Conflict and Progress: Fifty Years of Race Relations in South Africa* (Johannesburg: MacMillan South Africa, 1979), p. 173.

techniques. This leads to a loss of respect from students and parents, and to a loss of self-respect. The secondary teacher suffers from debilitatingly low morale. Black education is accordingly characterized by antiquated pedagogy (rote and textbook learning), low standards in mathematics and science instruction, and general underachievement. According to Dr. Kenneth B. Hartshorne, a former Department of Education and Training official, half of all African pupils leave school by age fourteen, many of them functionally illiterate.[17] The dropout rate is staggering and easily calculated from official data. About 31,000 standard ten (matric level) African students in 1980 were all that remained of more than 600,000 students who began grade one in 1968. That is little better than a 5 percent completion rate. Of those South Africans who began school in 1963 and completed twelve years of schooling, 58.4 percent were white, 22.3 percent were Indian, 4.4 percent were Coloured, and 1.96 percent were African.[18]

17. See Hartshorne, "Unfinished Business: Education for South Africa's Black People," p. 31. Critics of Nationalist educational policy also emphasize that one-third of all African students attend "farm schools" (4,800 of them), in which the government pays teacher salaries and sets the syllabus but white farmers determine the level of education offered and who can enroll.

18. *Rand Daily Mail*, October 9, 1981, featuring highlights of the de Lange Committee findings.

Resentment against what Africans still view as inferior "Bantu education" finds expression in chronic though episodic student strikes and parental resistance to the government's plans for introducing compulsory education. Initiated in the 1981 school year in 202 schools in 39 school districts for some 40,000 first-year students, compulsory education subject to local community approval faces an uncertain future. In addition to doubting the program's quality, parents fear that the legal obligation it imposes on them to see that their children continue in school may pit them against children who choose (as thousands do) to boycott classes in protest against what they perceive as imposed "Bantu education."

Qualitatively, South African schools are clearly not now able to prepare African students for careers in professions for which the country's manpower demands are and will be high, e.g., engineering, electronics, management. Top-level officials publicly acknowledge the need for qualitative improvement—though lower-level bureaucrats often obstruct efforts so aimed. In late 1976, then Minister of Bantu Education M. C. Botha stated that his department had not only adopted the same curricula and syllabuses as were used by whites, but black and white students were now writing the same senior certificate matriculation examination. He announced new programs to provide free textbooks for primary and secondary schools, establish adult education centers in African townships, and schedule the construction of new teacher training colleges, technical schools, and industrial training centers.[19]

The government has also stated that it intends to phase in equal pay for all teachers with similar qualifications. In 1981, salary parity was introduced at some administrative levels and the Department of Education and Training expressed its hope that financial circumstances in 1982 might permit it to expand this reform more broadly to the ranks of African teachers. If

19. Statement by M. C. Botha, December 29, 1976, quoted in RSA, Department of Information publication, *Bantu*, March 1977. For a discussion of efforts to improve Soweto schools since the student rioting of 1976 see Document I.

this policy for achieving pay scale equality is carried out, teaching will become a more attractive profession for Africans. That, in turn, may help to improve the quality of African education and thus to increase the number of Africans qualifying for university education.

Though this new thrust in African primary and secondary education seems likely to continue and presages a new era in higher education as well, the cumulative gap between white and African education remains enormous. Spending on African education has risen sharply—from R27 million in 1972–73 to R249 million in 1980–81[20]—then R369 million in 1981–82. As of now, however, the government still spends approximately ten times as much on a white as on an African student.[21] Educational spokesman for the liberal (Progressive Federal Party) parliamentary opposition Dr. Alex Boraine estimates that expenditures per white pupil in 1980–81 averaged R1,071 versus R113 per African student. This amounted to less than 1 percent of the Gross Domestic Product (GDP) for African education. If African education were to be placed on a par with white education, Boraine estimates, it would require an expenditure in excess of 10 percent of the GDP. Such an investment would require major budget shifts in favor of education, or a politically even more difficult cut in per capita expenditure on white students.

It is within this political-economic context that one must consider Prime Minister Botha's commitment to "equal education for all population groups"—a commitment qualified by the caveat that "the historical backlog cannot be erased overnight."[22] It is difficult to assess such commitment in the absence of a national consensus on what might constitute "equal education for all." Can segregated education be equal? And does the govern-

---

20. The rand (R) being roughly equivalent to the dollar. See statement by G. J. Rousseau, Director General, Department of Education and Training, in press release issued by RSA, Department of Foreign Affairs, Pretoria, October 14, 1980.

21. See *Survey of Race Relations in South Africa, 1980* (Johannesburg: South African Institute of Race Relations, 1981), p. 460.

22. Press statement, May 5, 1980; quoted in *Rand Daily Mail* (Extra), June 3, 1981.

ment commitment extend to erasing the historical backlog within a reasonable, specified period of time?

It was inevitable that a pressing need for coherent national policies to guide educational development would give rise to intense public debate. For example, during 1978–81, the South African Institute of Race Relations (SAIRR) made a case for new, integrative policies to promote equality of educational opportunity in a study entitled *Education for a New Era*;[23] the University of Witwatersrand staged a special lecture series on *South Africa's Crisis in Education*;[24] a group of prominent black educators met and formed a Council for Black Education and Research to develop a community-based agenda for the improvement of black education;[25] and the University of Cape Town organized a National Conference on Curriculum Innovation in South Africa.[26]

Most importantly, in June 1980, the government mandated the independent but state-funded Human Sciences Research Council (HSRC) to carry out an ambitious one-year investigation of South African education and to recommend:

☐ policies that could enable all South Africans to realize their individual potential, achieve economic growth, and improve the quality of their lives;

☐ policies to match organization, control, finance, and decision-making processes and manpower training priorities to the above goals;

23. For the text see Document II.

24. For the texts of three lectures on "Identity, Culture, and Curriculum," see Document III.

25. See Document IV.

26. Conference papers that focused on *Some Aspects of the Educational Crisis in the Western Cape in 1980* (C. J. Miller and S. Philcox, eds.) were published in January 1981 by the Center for Extra Mural Studies, University of Cape Town. In 1976, the University of Cape Town sponsored a conference on the role of universities in Southern Africa. Papers (mimeographed) included: J. Deganaar, "The Concept of a Volksuniversiteit;" J. Moulder, "University Neutrality: Some Puzzling Reflections in a South African Mirror;" E. Shils, "The Academic Ethos;" L. Thompson, "Some Problems of Southern African Universities;" and G. van N. Viljoen, "The Afrikaans Universities and Particularism."

□ programs designed to achieve "education of equal quality for all population groups."[27]

Professor J. P. de Lange, Rector of the Rand Afrikaans University (RAU), a former schoolteacher and prominent Afrikaner academic, directed the HSRC study.[28] Heading up a select committee of 25 academics that included significant black membership, de Lange mobilized the research energies of 800 scholars, organized workshops throughout the country, visited the technology-oriented educational systems of Israel and Taiwan, focused team labor around eighteen areas of investigation and, then, distilled forty thousand words of research team findings into a 220-page, jargon-packed report synthesizing a hammered-out committee consensus.[29] With a small army of translators and typists, he readied the bilingual report for the print-

27. See *Report of the National Manpower Commission*, p. 57.

28. Some academics see the government as using the HSRC to co-opt scholars into state-formulated research designed to expedite and legitimize government policy. The HSRC's role as a funding agency for university research, they believe, is thus confounded with the role of "promoter of government policy." Professor A. W. Stadler, head of the University of Witwatersrand Political Science Department, so argues in an unpublished memorandum shared with the USSALEP team. He fears that such disciplines as psychology, political science, sociology, and social anthropology will become instruments of political repression, serving the South African government as they served Stalinist Russia, American forces in Vietnam, and Latin American counter-insurgency.

"In the period of crisis and change through which this society is passing, and in the climate of increasing political control over independent, unorthodox, and critical opinion," writes Stadler, "it is critical that the universities should continue to function independently from state control over research and technology." University social scientists must be left free to "clarify, explain, and elucidate social and political phenomena" in their own methodical fashion. "It is tempting to demand of the universities that they should suspend the effort to understand, and offer the state solutions in the hour of crisis. But, as the political theorist Bertrand de Jouvenel pointed out, what characterizes a political problem is that no answer will fit the terms of the problem as stated; it can only be settled. The universities do not possess the means to settle the state's problems."

29. Main Committee of the HSRC Investigation into Education, *Education Provision in the RSA* (Pretoria: Human Sciences Research Council, July 1981). For the text of the report's recommended program for attaining "Education of Equal Quality for all Inhabitants," see Document V.

er's deadline and delivered it to the government in July 1981, just one year after its commission. It ranged in scope from prescriptive studies of how to foster preschool learning at home to recommendations concerning special bridging programs to enable more students to pursue university work in science and mathematics.

Extraordinary industry, publicity, and suspense surrounded the conduct of the study. When it was completed, de Lange held a series of confidential "seminars" explaining its findings to the cabinet. De Lange's personal vision reflected an Afrikaner cultural propensity to stereotype Africans as part of a group culture of subjective time, oral (versus "external") memory, and weak quantitative ("three-dimensional") reasoning. Nonetheless, through a process of pragmatic, integrative deliberation, he and his committee came to agree on the need for a more open educational system. They recommended creation of a single department of education; compulsory primary education and parity of expenditure on all school children as soon as possible; administrative decentralization with school admissions open on a basis of local or regional option ("regions" yet to be constitutionally defined); and establishment of a multiracial Council of Education to implement the committee's manifold recommendations for comprehensive educational development. For higher education the committee recommended that university councils rather than government determine whom (racially) to admit as students.

The government released the de Lange committee report in early October 1981. Simultaneously it issued a white paper that endorsed a list of general, hortatory principles for educational policy set forth by the committee but also stipulated a number of chilling "reservations." The white paper reaffirmed Nationalist commitment to the "Christian and national character" of education, the "principle of mother tongue" instruction, and the policy of separate schools and departments of education for "each population group." Instead of a Council of Education made up of distinguished educators and other community leaders, the government charged three cabinet ministers (National

Education, Education and Training, Internal Affairs) with responsibility for coordinating "consideration and possible implementation" of de Lange committee recommendations and invited all interested persons and organizations to submit comments to the Department of National Education by March 31, 1982.[30]

Meanwhile, the Minister of Education and Training, Dr. Ferdinand Hartzenberg, successfully pressed for parliament to create a new, black (principally African) multicampus university known as Vista to be headquartered near Pretoria and administered by his department.[31] This action conflicted with the spirit of the de Lange committee recommendations. It represented a victory for imposed, separatist education as opposed to voluntarist, community-based education. It constituted a bitter defeat for open institutions such as the University of Witwatersrand that wish to respond to black educational needs within a multiracial context.

The question of open versus ethnic is one of the most highly charged issues facing South African higher education. It is the most debated among a cluster of issues concerning the appropriateness of South Africa's institutions of higher learning. In light of the need for broadly expanded access to quality education, how do these institutions measure up?

I. Open Versus Ethnic

Arguably the most important questions about the appropriateness to South Africa's needs of its present and future institutions of higher education concern their ethnic character. To what de-

30. RSA, *Interim Memorandum: Provisional Comments by the Government on the Report of the Human Sciences Research Council on the Inquiry into the Provision of Education in the RSA*, October, 1981. For text see Document VI.

31. As parliament prepared to finalize its approval of Vista, the governing Council of the University of Witwatersrand warned that tight ministerial control would doom it to a stunted, inferior academic status. The Vista legislation (Vista University Bill, B73-81), in fact, ensured ministerial control over appointment, promotion, and discharge of key faculty and staff as well as over admission of non-blacks. *Rand Daily Mail*, September 16, 1981. In a detailed "Memorandum on the Vista University Bill" (August 11, 1981),

gree should or will South Africa's universities and other tertiary institutions deliberately cultivate an ethnic character—whether ethnically exclusive or heterogeneous? Who will decide how the country's ethnic diversity will be reflected in its educational institutions—the white minority or the affected institutions and groups? Universities themselves, though all constrained by apartheid law, vary in the degree to which they attempt to open their doors to all communities.

Responding to the de Lange committee report in advance of its publication, Minister of National Education Gerrit Viljoen warned that the government will not, in fact, allow an "unqualified" opening of universities and technikons to all races.[32] He indicated a willingness to review present procedures under which the government grants university and technikon entrance on a case by case basis to persons outside ascribed population groups. And there appears to be some sentiment within the government for allowing universities and technikons to admit students freely within government-fixed racial quotas. But there is also some fear among critics that Vista, once created as a multicampus, black township university, will provide the government with a rationale for reducing the number of already difficult to obtain permits for blacks who wish to attend open white universities.[33]

A recent survey of African matriculants in Transvaal showed that for reasons of quality and social contact, 75 percent would like to attend a [white] institution such as the University of Witwatersrand, while 87 percent rejected the very concept of segregated, black urban universities.[34] Minister of Education and

Principal Stuart J. Saunders of the University of Cape Town similarly argued that the Vista legislation would create a racially restrictive, government-dominated institution.

32. *Star*, September 1, 1981.

33. In the period from March 1, 1978 to April 20, 1979, 1,700 Africans applied to study at universities other than those to which Africans are legally assigned. Of these applicants, 347 received permission. For Coloureds, the comparable figures were 644 requests and 592 permissions. *Survey of Race Relations in South Africa, 1979*, pp. 545–546.

34. A survey of 500 African students conducted by Witwatersrand sociologist Mark Orkin. *Star*, August 19, 1981.

Training Ferdinand Hartzenberg, by contrast, stressed the historic significance of creating the first university for Africans to be situated within a "white area" as distinct from a homeland. Thus seen, Vista represents a tacit admission of the permanence of the country's urban African population.

As an alternative to the imposed segregation of Vista, educational leaders such as Professor Es'kia Mphahlele (Witwatersrand) and Principal Stuart J. Saunders (Cape Town) have advocated the establishment of autonomous community colleges modeled on those of the United States. With help from and as bridges to universities, such colleges could offer a wide range of service programs, including courses to upgrade underqualified teachers.[35] If built on a voluntary community base, they would be free from the taint of "Bantu education" and could serve burgeoning needs that predominantly white universities, even if fully "open," cannot.[36] So far the government has been unreceptive.

South Africa's traditionally elite English-medium universities now enroll four times as many African, Coloured, and Indian students as they did before the Nationalist government enacted strict racial bars in the mid-1950s. Their capacity to meet a rapidly increasing African demand for higher education, however, remains limited. The willingness of government officials to permit some blacks to attend white institutions has yet to be matched by a general willingness on the part of Afrikaans-medium universities to open their doors to Afrikaans-speaking Coloureds, let alone to Africans. The stigma of their being created under apartheid makes it difficult for black institutions to achieve academic prestige or to establish supportive links abroad. Even universities within "independent" homelands

35. As one argument for establishing Vista, the government cited a need to provide local educational opportunities for 33,654 teachers, of whom only 448 had university degrees. Ibid.

36. Imposed racial segregation and tight government control, rather than projected part-time, remedial, non-degree, or odd-hour programming, have caused the sharp criticism of Vista. For Professor Mphahlele's arguments in favor of black community colleges, see Document VII; and for the memo of Dr. Saunders and the University of Cape Town, see Document X.

where racial restrictions on education have been lifted experience continued isolation because their governments are internationally ostracized. The fact remains that these new and expanding black universities, even if declared racially open, must primarily serve the growing needs of South Africa's black communities. A diverse spectrum of black institutions is emerging as an important force within South African higher education— a force with which all those who would foster expanded educational opportunity must reckon.

ENGLISH-MEDIUM UNIVERSITIES

Characteristically, South Africa's open universities foster intellectual ties abroad, maintain high standards of instruction and research, grant faculty an important role in governance and formation of educational policy, tolerate campus political dissent as expressed in part through Student Representative Councils (SRCs) and publications,[37] and enroll relatively heterogeneous

37. For example, the official SRC organ, *Wits Student*, regularly and roundly criticizes the Witwatersrand University administration and the government and praises student opposition to apartheid policies. A five-year banning order against the former "Wits" SRC president, Sammy Adelman, following a June 1981 on-campus flag burning incident, temporarily cooled overt political protest. Adelman's successor as SRC president, Jeremy Clark, declared heroics, romanticism, and the politics of protest "out." "After a year in which the Wits campus has seen riot police, flag burning, a demo[nstration] against Dr. Piet Koornhoff [Minister of Cooperation and Development], and the banning of student leaders, we've come to see the limits of reactive, protest-type activity." But Clark said that the Wits SRC should continue to work for democracy, by which he meant "majority rule." *Star* (September 4, 1981).

Similarly, in August 1981, Trevor Bailey, the SRC president at the University of Natal, called on Natal students to be more tolerant of "other people's views" while preparing themselves for useful roles in a nonracial South Africa—"the arrival of which is inevitable." *Natal Mercury* (Durban), August 28, 1981.

University student dissent gets considerable attention in the English-language press. On August 18, 1981, the *Star* published interviews with five former Wits SRC presidents. Interviewer Jasper Mortimer commented that student leaders had greater success in "eroding apartheid" after leaving the university. They go on "to take up important positions in unions, tutorial colleges, legal aid societies, and literacy schools." The Legal Resources Center of Johannesburg, for instance, is staffed by three ex-leaders of the National Union of South African Students (NUSAS).

TABLE 3
Students by Race

	White	Coloured	Indian	Chinese	Black (African)	Totals
Arts	2806	55	144	7	39	3051
Science	1402	34	167	35	52	1690
Medicine	1804	33	136	35	44	2052
Engineering	1739	13	29	11	77	1869
Commerce	2544	24	86	90	24	2768
Law	620	7	67	4	39	737
Dentistry	399	2	18	7	4	430
Architecture	403	2	15	3	27	450
Education	589	13	48	–	30	680
Business Administration	405	–	6	3	24	438
TOTALS	12711	183	716	195	360	14165

student bodies. Just how heterogeneous the Witwatersrand student body has become is illustrated by the 1981 profile shown in Tables 3 and 4. (See Document X for Cape Town enrollment data.)

Relatively high financial costs, inadequate residential facilities and transportation, and "problems of being at a university dominated by students of another culture and home language" will continue to limit "Wits" black student enrollments. But Johannesburg's open university has adopted a long-term academic plan that calls both for a multiracial enrollment of 22,000 and an increased number of black faculty and senior staff. Prepared under the guidance of its liberal surgeon-principal, Dr. D. J. du Plessis, the Witwatersrand plan prescribes the mission of an open university in contemporary South Africa.

The Academic Plan recognises that although Wits has freely admitted students of all races and classes, and has vigorously resisted restrictions which have been imposed on this freedom, we have historically served predominantly the white middle class community of the Witwatersrand. We must now strengthen our efforts to become a university which is effectively open to all of those who

TABLE 4
Students by Sex and Full-time or Part-time Status

	Male	Female	Full-time	Part-time
Arts	1047	2004	2853	198
Science	1046	644	1532	158
Medicine	1255	797	1978	74
Engineering	1815	54	1634	235
Commerce	2329	439	1528	1240
Law	578	159	408	329
Dentistry	384	46	354	76
Architecture	376	74	431	19
Education	225	455	553	127
Business Administration	367	71	119	319
TOTALS	9422	4733	11390	2775

SOURCE: University of Witwatersrand.

are qualified and wish to receive a university education in the English language. Some students, who have high innate abilities but have suffered from poor home backgrounds or inadequate schooling, will initially need special help if they are to benefit fully from the type of education we offer. This adds a new dimension to our activities, but, if we are energetic and skillful, it will not weaken the best of the things we do today, and could well enrich them by adding new ideas and new colleagues. Combining strong liberal and technological traditions, and situated in the industrial hub of the most advanced nation of Africa, Wits is in a unique position to contribute to [solving] some of the major problems of modern society.[38]

To the south at the University of Cape Town (UCT), Principal Stuart Saunders has eloquently articulated the ideals, hopes,

38. Professor F. R. N. Nabarro (Deputy Vice-Chancellor), "An Outline of the Academic Plan" (Johannesburg: University of Witwatersrand, 1980). For less orthodox ideas coming out of Wits on what South African universities should be, see Document VIII.

The case of Dr. Norman Ferrandi of the Wits mathematics department is illustrative of how some individual faculty at open universities serve the needs of black educational development. The USSALEP team found him spending his sabbatical leave working with a program in Soweto to upgrade mathematics teachers.

and problems of the open university[39] and brought his campus to address concrete issues of how to render itself more accessible to black students. Two means being tried: (1) a "cadet scheme" for black students under which the university provides special academic support while prospective employers pay tuition and living costs; and (2) a part-time, after-hours teacher training degree program. Both are the kind of initiatives that require outside financial support.[40]

To the east, the University of Natal (Durban) administers a black medical school (300 African, 300 Indian) and enrolls another 600 to 700 blacks (largely Indian). In the person of its Principal, Professor N. D. Clarence, Natal stands for multiracial education. Clarence is an outspoken advocate of a single department of education with a "uniform philosophy" and policies aimed at achieving equality of educational opportunity "as quickly as possible."[41]

In general, black students are hard put to manage the logistics of commuting to white universities. At Witwatersrand the Black Student Society rents a bus to serve Indian townships 40 miles outside Johannesburg. A few black students are quietly accommodated at or near open universities. Yet despite vacancies in residences at UCT the government has consistently refused to permit blacks to occupy them. Frustrated UCT administrators decided to risk the construction of special hostel facilities.

Student informers, political arrests, interracial tensions—all linked to intense government interest in and disapproval of multiracial education—also serve to discourage blacks from attending open English-medium universities. Nevertheless, the

39. See Document IX.
40. See Document X. In the Eastern Cape, a small number of blacks attend Rhodes University (Grahamstown). Rhodes' enrollment in 1980 was 2,701 White; 53 Coloured; 82 Indian; 35 Chinese; 44 African; 2,915 total.
41. *Sunday Tribune* (Durban), July 12, 1981. In 1980 University of Natal enrollment was 7,547 White; 179 Coloured; 656 Indian; 13 Chinese; 376 African; 8,771 total. The university features several strong research programs, including an internationally respected Institute for Social Research headed by Dr. Lawrence Schlemmer and extensive scientific research projects in the Antarctic.

academic prestige, relative intellectual freedom, and social conscience of these universities[42] constitute a powerful attraction.

AFRIKAANS-MEDIUM UNIVERSITIES

Ethno-linguistic in origins and rationale, Afrikaans-medium universities remain largely homogeneous and closed. The University of Pretoria, a fifty-year-old, 18,000-student citadel of Afrikaner traditionalism admits no black students.[43] Its largely conservative faculty, which includes Professor Carel Boshoff, head of the secret Broederbond society,[44] persists in viewing South Africa as a collection of distinct nations whose educational systems ought to remain separate. The official *University of Pretoria Information Brochure* (p. 37) numbers the white administrative, faculty, and technical staff at 2,251, then adds: "The University has a black labour force of 1,145, whose duties consist mainly of cleaning the buildings and maintaining the grounds."

Radiating the confidence of a people who have secured political and economic ascendency and have become cautiously more outward looking, the faculty and students of the University of Pretoria and other Afrikaans universities enjoy excellent facilities, generous funding, a rich faculty-student ratio (1 to 14 at Pretoria) and, amongst them, a full range of graduate and professional schools.[45] Graduates, including an increasing pro-

42. See L. J. Suzman, ed., *The Rights and Responsibilities of Universities in Contemporary Society* (A series of special lectures given at the University of Witwatersrand in July through August 1973).

43. An exception was made for two black graduate students allowing them to enroll in the Faculty of Veterinary Science, given the absence of any black alternative. About 10 percent of Pretoria's students are English-speaking and may take examinations in either English or Afrikaans.

44. So identified by the press (*Sunday Tribune*, August 23, 1981), Professor Boshoff, in conversation with the USSALEP team, lauded the continuing hold of religion on young Afrikaners despite secular trends in contemporary society.

45. Under the direction of its principal, D. M. Joubert, the University of Pretoria has developed a solid capacity for institutional research. Its staff is investigating the causes of a first-year student drop-out rate of 30 to 35 percent and exploring how this attrition may be related to deficiencies in housing, academic advising, and preparation in basic mathematics and science.

portion of women, enjoy easy access to careers in the civil service and industry.

In Johannesburg, the Afrikaner community acquired its own Rand Afrikaans University (RAU) in 1967. An expandable, modular pile of well-equipped, cavernous buildings with some 5,200 largely (63 percent) commuter students (over half of them in education), RAU is a true *volksuniversiteit*.[46] Under its Rector, J. P. de Lange, RAU is growing at an annual rate of some 14 percent, is regularly adding new faculties (engineering is the latest) and is planning for a student body of 15,000 by the year 2000. To this end it relies not only on government funds but energetically raises funds within the urban Afrikaner community. Concerning other communities, RAU enrolls some English-speakers (12 percent), admitted 11 black graduate students in 1981, and has quietly conducted an upgrading course for 300 black schoolteachers. But RAU remains only slightly less closed than Pretoria.

As at other Afrikaans-medium universities, RAU's relatively benign Student Representative Council (SRC) presents no major problems for the administration. Its respectful, well-dressed students contrast with the bumptious, blue-jeaned undergraduates of nearby Wits.

Reflecting a certain polarization within the Afrikaner community, the Political Student Society (Polstu), a dissident, liberal Afrikaner student group critical of government racial policy, recently entered the Afrikaans university scene.[47] Its 500 or so members, however, represent only a miniscule portion of the 38,000 students at RAU and the other Afrikaans universities

46. *Volksuniversiteit*: a university centered in an ethnic group. See J. Degenaar, "The Concept of a Volksuniversiteit" (mimeographed paper delivered at conference on the Role of Universities in Southern Africa, Cape Town, 1976). See also Document XI.

47. See *New York Times*, July 11, 1981. The conservative mainstream of Afrikaner student politics is represented on university campuses by the *Afrikanse Studentbond* (ASB).

and their emergence is being matched by a parallel growth of organized, ultra–right wing sentiment.

In the south, at the fount of Afrikaner intellectualism, the University of Stellenbosch, a perceptibly more open, less consensual spirit prevails. Endowed with a panoply of quality research institutes, Stellenbosch boasts that it attracts "the best students in the country"—including a half-dozen who became prime ministers. About 12.5 percent come from English-speaking families. Stressing the importance of maintaining the Afrikaner character of the institution, including traditional student respect for parental and professional authority, however, the Stellenbosch SRC told the USSALEP team that it would not want that percentage to increase appreciably.[48]

In 1977 Stellenbosch announced that it was opening its doors to a limited number of black (mostly Coloured) graduate students. Though obliged to live off campus in nearby black townships, some 100 blacks are now enrolled. In cooperation with the South African Institute of Race Relations, the Genesis Foundation of the United States decided to offer scholarships to black Stellenbosch students beginning in 1982. And though faculty and student advocates of open undergraduate enrollment at the beautiful 12,000-student campus have not yet prevailed, Rector Mike de Vries has publicly declared himself in favor of placing admission to all universities, technikons, and teacher training colleges on a basis of strictly academic (nonracial) qualifications.[49]

Stellenbosch is a center of liberal Afrikaans thought. Professor Willie Esterhuyse, head of the Department of Social and

48. SRC members expressed concern and bewilderment that black students (including Afrikaans-speaking students of the University of the Western Cape) refuse to attend intercampus meetings where student representatives of Stellenbosch are present. They lamented: "We do not want to be incommunicado."

49. *Christian Science Monitor*, July 3, 1981. For Professor de Vries' views on higher education in South Africa see Document XII.

Political Philosophy, is a frequent contributor to the Calvinist journal *Woord en Daad* and author of the spirited and controversial *Apartheid Must Die*.[50] Another Stellenbosch voice for racial accommodation is anthropologist Christof Hanekom. He argues that Afrikaners should see in black Africans' political assertion a "reflected image" of their own. "Because we have escaped from the bonds of colonialism and cultural enslavement, we ourselves qualify to assist the black man in this southernmost part of Africa with advice and material aid in order that he may also gain his freedom."[51] In keeping with this sentiment, the Stellenbosch Faculty of Education is reaching out, cooperating in a teacher training program with the University of Zululand and working with projects to improve Coloured education (most of the 2.6 million Cape Coloured are Afrikaans-speaking).

COLOURED AND INDIAN UNIVERSITIES

Coloured university students were assigned to the University of the Western Cape under the apartheid legislation of 1959. It is ethnic and closed.

Located in a Coloured township outside of Cape Town, Western Cape enrolls 3,500 students. Its Rector, Professor R. E. van der Ross, author of the perceptive study *Myths and Attitudes: An Inside Look at the Coloured People*,[52] is an ardent believer in computer technology as an instructional tool. In an effort to mobilize technology to help underprepared students bridge their way into university-level work, he led Western Cape to invest in sixty-four Plato terminals programmed for instruction in applied mathematics, physics, chemistry, statistics, computer sci-

50. Translated from the original Afrikaans and published by Tafelberg, Cape Town, 1981. Another prominent contributor to *Woord en Daad*, Professor J. H. Coetzee of the University of Potchefstroom, recently used that journal to warn Nationalists that "the Afrikaner still has a chance to participate in an all-race government or [alternatively to] be pushed out of any effective participation in the political revolution." "We must make the choice before someone else does it for us." *Sunday Times* (Johannesburg), August 30, 1981.

51. Christoff Hanekom, "South Africa: The Present and the Future," mimeograph, University of Stellenbosch, 1981.

52. Published by Tafelberg, Cape Town, 1979.

ence, languages, and other subjects.[53] The university has also sought community relatedness through an Institute for Social Development to promote regional socioeconomic research and through an Institute for Historical Research focused on the history of race relations throughout South Africa.[54]

The educational climate of Western Cape, however, is suffused with bitter student and faculty alienation from the university as a creature of apartheid. The University has been opposed by the Coloured community as an ethnic institution: "Students initially came under protest but now come to protest." Since they resent being assigned to a racially segregated university, which they view as a pawn of white authority, some students refuse to use campus athletic facilities because they are superior to those of their community. In the view of the student chaplain, Rev. Allan Boesak, an alumnus of Union Theological Seminary in New York and a perceptive social analyst, if community leadership rather than a white government ministry controlled the university and its curriculum, ethnic homogeneity would be widely accepted as educationally appropriate.

Instead, dissident social thought flourishes beneath Western Cape's deceptively decorous academic surface. The official

53. Dr. van der Ross, who described installation of the Plato system as "possibly the most important single step taken in the improvement of teaching methods since the establishment of [Western Cape] university twenty years ago," is a vocal advocate of pedagogical reform in grade school. The accent, he argues, should be on "exploration and discovery, developing of concepts and of reasoning powers rather than of memorisation." *UWC News* 6, no. 1, April 1981.

54. South African history books are "mainly 'white-centered.' " Therefore, the Institute for Historical Research "wants to make a particular contribution in this field by cultivating among the various population groups a lively interest in the past, especially in the race relationship situation." It is mandated "to inform" but not "to prescribe." University of the Western Cape, *1981 General Catalog*, Part 1, p. 28.

Social science research on contemporary South African race relations is centered at the nearby Abe Bailey Institute of Race Relations of the University of Cape Town. That Institute's publications include studies of Coloured society. See for example, Hendrik W. van der Merwe and C. J. Groenewald, eds., *Occupational and Social Change Among Coloured People in South Africa* (Cape Town: Juta, 1976).

1981 catalog opens with a description of proper faculty and student ceremonial dress: for the Principal, "a peony red gown with full facing and yoke of spectrum blue velvet, edged with silver lace and open sleeves looped up with a silver cord and lined with blue satin." Although shut down in 1977, the Student Representative Council (SRC) has been revived, and it is almost certain to collide repeatedly with authority. Unless and until Coloured South Africans regain enfranchised citizenship, the University of the Western Cape seems fated to reflect the torment of a rejected people.

By law Indian university students are supposed to study at the University of Durban-Westville. Opened in 1961 to service a diverse Indian community (70 percent Hindu, 20 percent Muslim, and 10 percent Christian), Durban-Westville is viewed with a mixture of doubt and resignation by its 5,000 students.[55]

Upwardly mobile, Indian students worry that a degree from an ethnic university must lack the career-enhancing prestige of a degree from an open university. In the words of a young Indian faculty member who was leaving to accept a position at the neighboring University of Natal: "Students have never accepted the idea of an all-Indian university. They see it as an apartheid institution, worry about its reputation, believe that no one who can teach elsewhere will teach at it. They don't know that there are third-rate lecturers at Wits. They have no basis for comparison." Accordingly, students protest, condemning the institution to chronic disruption and further reducing its academic attractiveness.

Since 1978, however, a special act of parliament has allowed Durban-Westville to admit more non-Indian students. The new Faculty of Health Sciences has enrolled some 10 Africans, 50 Coloureds, and 50 whites. An official brochure, *University of Durban-Westville*, foresees a multiracial campus of 10,000 by 1990—"one of the best universities in South Africa . . . with absolutely first-class facilities for study, research, recreation, and community involvement."

55. About 2,000 Indians are studying at other residential universities.

The founding Rector, Dr. S. P. Olivier, is a low-profile Afrikaner, but the faculty is relatively cosmopolitan—nearly 40 percent Indian with others from Europe, Asia, and even the United States. The faculty-student ratio is a favorable 1 to 15. The academic program features law, education, and engineering along with Indian languages and cultures. In an Indian community of seven hundred ninety-two thousand, some two hundred thirty-three thousand of whom are enrolled in an educational program, the University of Durban-Westville has come to perceive itself as "the most important single factor in establishing the Indian minority group as a powerful, creative force in industry, commerce, and the professions."[56]

AFRICAN UNIVERSITIES

The campuses of Durban-Westville and the neighboring University of Natal peer from suburban hilltops over adjacent middle class constituencies. Contrastingly, the rural black campuses of segregated African universities lie far from major population centers well out in the African "bush." If the government's intent has been to insulate them from the sociopolitical ferment of black urban life, however, it has not been successful. For example, the University of the North is situated on an isolated farm, Turfloop, twenty-five miles from the nearest town, Pietersburg. A visitor to the campus quickly senses a pervasive, cloistered tension. The university has no functioning Student Representative Council (SRC). It has no student publications. Its rector is African, Professor P. C. Mokgokong, but the faculty consists largely of Afrikaners educated at ethnically particularist universities such as Pretoria and Potchefstroom. The university's one research publication is a scholastic theological journal which rarely refers to African churches or society.[57] Of the uni-

56. *University of Durban-Westville* (Durban, 1981).

57. *Theologia Viatorum,* Journal of the Faculty of Theology, University of the North. Some faculty members, however, do carry out applied research of relevance to the African community. For example, both Turfloop and the University of Zululand host research projects in pisciculture that should have positive economic and dietary spinoffs. In 1979, the university hosted a symposium on education and socioeconomic development in Lebowa, the African

versity's 3,000 students, 98 percent live on campus. Sixty percent drop out by the end of their first year (there is no research to explain why), and large numbers of students collide with authority in foredoomed annual political demonstrations that lead to a further winnowing of student ranks. The USSALEP team found little evidence of efforts to meet the patent need for remedial or bridging programs. Until this need is recognized and acted upon at Turfloop and the other African universities, African student bodies will, perforce, be afflicted with high attrition, underachievement, and low morale.

Although the University of the North offers a broad curriculum, with faculty and laboratories for highly specialized training in such fields as optometry and pharmacology, few of its students have been adequately prepared for university-level science. More of them turn to public administration and economics, preparing themselves for careers as homeland administrators. And the University of the North is itself engaged in furthering homeland development by helping to found the nuclei of new universities in the mini-homelands of Venda and Qwaqwa.[58]

With each homeland intent on having its own university, fledgling African universities are fated to compete for faculty from an almost drained pool of modest talent. In the absence of black Ph.D.s, the proliferation of these institutions provides ca-

homeland within which it is located. The proceedings were published in *Educational Priorities in a Developing State* (Symposium held by the Association of Inspectors of Education in Lebowa, January 9–11, 1979; Pretoria: de Jager-Haum, 1979).

58. Interviewed at the University of Transkei, where he headed the Department of Mathematics, the Rector-elect of the University of Qwaqwa, Professor W. Mödinger (Ph.D. Stuttgart, West Germany) expressed the hope that his embryonic institution could avoid the history of unrest that has chronically disrupted education at Turfloop. Some students at Turfloop and Fort Hare actually sought confrontation, Professor Mödinger argued, because they preferred to be thrown out before they flunked out. Mödinger indicated that Qwaqwa would emphasize bridging courses and applied sciences, stress teacher education and non-degree work in community-relevant fields such as agriculture and electronics. Commenting on the fragmented nature of South African education and society, Mödinger observed that it resembles Germany at the time of the Holy Roman Empire.

reer opportunities for Afrikaner Ph.D.s unable to obtain posts in white institutions. Inevitably, however, these academics bring with them ethnocentric values and a defensive self-perception of second-class status that works against the development of African-centered intellectual quality and institutional pride.

At the University of Zululand, the Rector, Professor A. C. Nkabinde, is trying, despite a preponderance of Afrikaner faculty and staff, to develop and adapt his university to the status of an open yet African-centered institution.[59] On the University's 2,500-student Empangeni campus near the developing port city of Richards Bay, the field of black education enjoys top priority.[60] Acquisition of a four-hundred-acre plot of land will permit the addition of agricultural studies designed to help Zulu peasants upgrade the productivity of traditional farming. To train African students in social science and research techniques and thereby generate a new resource for regional development, Professor Absolom Vilikazi (formerly Professor of Anthropology at American University, Washington, D.C.) has founded a Center for Social Research and Documentation. Dr. Vilikazi expressed to the USSALEP team an eagerness to have American, especially black American, professors, or advanced graduate students in such fields as demography pursue combined research and instructional projects at his Center. In a similar vein, Rector Nkabinde stated that he had repeatedly but unsuccessfully urged the U.S. International Cooperation Agency (ICA) to send academic specialists in communications skills and science teaching to lecture and consult at South African institutions such as the University of Zululand.

In his efforts to develop an African faculty, Nkabinde has turned to the University of Natal for provision of advanced graduate training. The Rector of Natal, Dr. N. D. Clarence, in turn has indicated support for a bilateral faculty exchange pro-

59. In September 1981, Dr. Nkabinde convened a symposium of educators to help define the goals of the University of Zululand. See Document XIII.

60. Education Professor P. C. Luthuli recently published an historical study, *The Philosophical Foundations of Black Education in South Africa* (Durban: Butterworths, 1981) that argues for an educational system sensitively adapted to the needs of changing African culture.

gram should funding become available. And the University of Natal has extended technical help as the University of Zululand has begun establishing an urban extension in the KwaZulu township of Umlazi, Durban. Some 350 part-time, mostly evening students are already taking courses at temporary Umlazi facilities.

Eager to serve needful African constituencies, educational leaders such as Professor Nkabinde face intimidating difficulties. How can the University of Zululand be considered in a genuine, or even inchoate, sense African when its history department is composed entirely of Afrikaner instructors formed intellectually within ethnocentric Afrikaans-medium institutions? How can it be considered community-oriented when its academically underprepared, black consciousness–prone students fear to expose themselves to political intimidation and thus refuse to elect a Student Representative Council? How can any black university claim academic distinction or even adequacy, when, after more than twenty years, its library contains less than one hundred thousand volumes in contrast to the three-hundred-thousand-volume, automated library of the much newer Rands Afrikaans University?[61]

Commenting on the role of black universities since 1959, the daily *Sowetan* (August 20, 1981) recently extended a backhanded compliment:

> Our experience of black universities is a somewhat interesting one. Despite the fact that students from Turfloop, Fort Hare, and Durban-Westville may have had an inferior type of education, they came out as some of the most articulate, in fact, the most dynamic political thinkers in years.
>
> In the hey-days of black consciousness, it can well be said that the ideology got its aggressive resurgence from what was derogatorily called the Bush College.
>
> People like the late Steve Biko cut their political teeth at these

---

61. Such is the impoverished status of the libraries at the University of the North, Durban-Westville, Fort Hare, Zululand, and Western Cape. A tour of the library at the University of the North revealed that, of its approximately one hundred thousand volumes, many are obsolete or otherwise useless—including dated and poor quality rejects from other libraries.

colleges, or through them. What happened appears easily understandable taken as hindsight.

Black students were not too dumb to be acutely aware they were being ripped off educationally and that their position was disadvantaged. They were receiving some insights from the world around them, and being presumably intelligent and serious young men and women, they drew their own conclusions. They went further by acting on these conclusions.

The government was caught trapped, and with its usual paucity of responses, banned, banished, and martyred those youngsters.

On the basis of this experience the *Sowetan* went on to predict that the creation of Vista, the government's new urban version of the "bush college," will lead to similar results. "We are not saying the same thing will automatically take off here, but the options for its recurring are manifold. Today's student is even more sensitive to being disadvantaged, and particularly responsive to action. We rather think we will be hearing a great deal more from them right on our doorstep."

Planned as a complex of township campuses administered from a Pretoria headquarters, Vista is supposed to serve the needs of part-time, nonresident students who want to study but cannot give up their jobs. In the words of Dr. J. G. Garbers, President of the Human Sciences Research Council (HSRC), the need is legitimate. Demand for higher education among urban blacks is rising. Seen as an extension of apartheid, however, Vista will assuredly meet derision and resistance. The root problem, Garbers notes, lies in the fact that blacks have no voice in formulating educational policy (viz. the importance of the de Lange Committee's proposal for a multiracial Council of Education).[62]

Consistent with these perceptions, though its facilities are modern and impressive, the new Medical University of South Africa (Medunsa) for blacks at Pretoria is currently scorned by African physicians educated at the University of Natal Medical School. As a creature of apartheid, Medunsa, they reason, can never expect to attract quality medical faculty of international stature. Some Africans believe that the government intends it precisely so.

62. *Christian Science Monitor*, October 20, 1981.

The fact remains that a significant number of resourceful young blacks rely on their own talent and persistence, make the best of their circumstances, and wrest a decent education from segregated black institutions. At isolated Turfloop, for example, the USSALEP team met poised, articulate students who reminded it of how segregated black colleges of circumscribed means long served the educational needs of black Americans to whom other institutions of higher learning were closed. Much of the black leadership of the civil rights movement that did so much to open up American society, higher education included, was educated at those black institutions.

HOMELAND UNIVERSITIES

But what about African universities being absorbed into or created by homelands which have accepted political "independence" from South Africa? Are they open or closed? What role will they play in the unfolding drama of South African higher education? Are they appropriate to their circumstances?

The once prestigious University of Fort Hare falls within the territory of the latest homeland to be bequeathed South African style independence. In becoming the university of a diminutive and impoverished Republic of Ciskei, Fort Hare, sadly, may suffer further decline. Ciskei seems unlikely to offer either the economic or political conditions necessary for a strong university or educational system.

With an assist from Fort Hare, the first independent homeland, Transkei, founded its own open university in 1976. Rising like the Château of Chambord from rolling fields outside Transkei's modest capital, Umtata, the University of Transkei, its construction and operational budget underwritten by South Africa, enrolls about 1,000 students. Though headed by an Afrikaner professor of education from Fort Hare, Dr. B. de V. van der Merwe, it has attracted a more diverse (55 to 60 percent black) faculty than have ethnic universities in South Africa "proper."[63] Its department of education is wrestling with the

63. To illustrate, the University of Transkei's department of history is headed by F. J. Mashasha (D.Phil., Oxford); political science by Gerhard K. H. Tötemeyer (D.Phil., Stellenbosch); religious studies by Rev. E. K. Moso-

daunting problem of how to upgrade teacher training colleges, develop special programs in science teaching, reform school pedagogy so as to foster critical thinking, and adapt and use video materials in schools and adult education programs. Given the unpreparedness of black students in mathematics and English, the university senate is considering the requirement of an extra (fourth) year—though there as elsewhere black students resist the notion of any arrangement that deviates from what is standard in white schools. So strong is the fear of regression to Bantu education that, despite the obvious need for bridging programs in such fields as mathematics and English, compensatory programs for blacks are automatically suspect. Failure rates are high—55 to 60 percent of those who enter the University of Transkei in public administration, for example. Out of 350 students who enter the sciences in a given year, some 50 graduate in three years, another 50 after an additional year.[64]

What gives the University of Transkei a certain vitality, despite grave weaknesses such as a library of just twenty-five thousand volumes and an absence of programs in computer sciences or agriculture, is the political latitude to relate to its African context. Like black universities officially within the Republic its fees are low (R250, plus R500 for room and board), but unlike them it has considerable leeway for curricular and research initiative. Illustrative is its new Institute for Management and Development Studies. Established to channel faculty research and training capabilities into concrete socioeconomic development projects, the Institute, headed by German economist Wolfgang H. Thomas, has begun publishing a *Transkei Development Review* and has organized a special "honors course" in Development Planning.[65] The Institute plans to focus training efforts in such

---

thoane (L.Th., Birmingham); law by D. F. L. Thompson (LL.B., Natal); education by J. M. Noruwana (Ed.D., Columbia); botany by A. J. Tew (Ph.D., Witwatersrand); and physics by K. Albrecht (Ph.D., Frankfort).

64. According to the former Dean of the Faculty of Science, W. Mödinger, who lamented the low level of science teaching and absence of practical laboratory experience in black schools.

65. For the course description and statement of editorial purpose from the *Review*, see Document XIV. The vice-chairman of the Institute's Man-

areas as low-cost housing and small business and rural development and is eager to establish links with American researchers
working in the field of development planning.

The concept of the university as agent of socioeconomic development is asserted even more saliently as the raison d'être of
the newest and most unorthodox homeland university, the
University of Bophuthatswana. With more hopeful economic
prospects (platinum, maize, cattle) than Ciskei or Transkei, the
geographically fragmented state of Bophuthatswana has established its university as the capstone of a restructured, community-oriented educational system. The university is mandated
to coordinate all higher education, including tertiary-level
schools of education, agriculture, and technology. The centrality and difficulty of its role in the refashioning of education in
Bophuthatswana has been emphasized by the chairman of its
University Council, Dr. Kenneth B. Hartshorne:

> The quality and attitudes of [teacher] training college staff [fac-
> ulty] leaves much to be desired and the response to the needs of
> the new dispensation in Bophuthatswana has been disappointing.
> It is for this reason that the present emphasis in curriculum devel-
> opment is on the curriculum of the training colleges and on the
> creation of professional leadership in these colleges. The full in-
> volvement of the University will be absolutely imperative in this
> enterprise, for in the human context of curriculum reform the
> teacher educator is the critical link. Fortunately, there are now
> clear signs that this is realized within the University and also by a
> growing number of the more receptive members of training col-
> lege staffs.[66]

Curricular innovation at the fledgling University of Bophuthatswana (UNIBO) itself may encounter internal as well as
external resistance. UNIBO emphasizes professional and
vocational studies, flexible admission policies, instructional ef-

---

agement Committee, Professor of Accountancy W. L. Nkuhlu, has been enabled by an IIE grant to pursue advanced graduate work at New York University.

66. Kenneth B. Hartshorne, "Curriculum and the Reality of Context: The
Bophuthatswana Beginnings" (Paper presented at Conference on Curriculum and Community, University of Witwatersrand, July 1980).

fectiveness, and special support and bridging programs for underprepared students. Only the hiring of an unusually able and dedicated faculty will enable the university to achieve the academic and community service goals that it has set for itself.[67] To assemble such a faculty will not be easy. Furthermore it may prove hard to wrench recognition of a Bophuthatswana degree from the orthodox leadership of South African higher education.[68]

Nonetheless, UNIBO's first chancellor, Sir Albert Robinson, has described it as a triumph for the ever-expanding cause of nonracialism in Southern Africa. Sir Albert, chairman of Johannesburg Consolidated Investment, provides a link with white capital and liberal sentiment. With an enrollment of 750 students that is expected to increase at a rate of 400 to 500 a year,[69] "UNIBO," he has declared, "is a nonracial institution established within a multiracial society which by its influence and example will help to erode racial domination and discrimination wherever it may be found."[70]

On paper, this new venture in African and Africa-oriented education comes the closest of any university in South Africa to meeting the criteria for institutional appropriateness as set forth by one of the country's most articulate young black intellects, Dr. N. Chabani Manganyi. A clinical psychologist who made the long journey from undergraduate at the University of the North to postgraduate student at Yale University, and ulti-

67. For a discussion of these goals see Document XV.
68. On the other hand, the University of Witwatersrand offered start-up assistance to UNIBO. It made its London office available to UNIBO officials seeking external linkages, and Witwatersrand faculty have served as consultants for faculty recruitments and the establishment of curricular standards.
69. As of 1981, students were divided among UNIBO's three campuses as follows: 110 at the agricultural branch, Taung; 570 (education, law, social work, health sciences, commerce) at the main campus in Mmabatho, the capital; 70 at the technical college, Ga-Rankuwa near Pretoria. Interview with Dr. Hartshorne.
70. Quoted from an address by Sir Albert on the occasion of the official opening of the University by Bophuthatswana President Lucas Mangope, *Rand Daily Mail*, September 14, 1981.

mately professor at the University of Witwatersrand, Dr. Manganyi addresses the issue of open versus ethnic universities with insight and passion. He rejects "universalism as professed by the English-medium universities" as inappropriate in the absence of a unified, democratic society. In aristocratically concentrating on ideals of autonomy and academic freedom impossible to achieve in today's South Africa, Manganyi writes, they fail to respond to the need to become *African* universities, they fail to recognize the realities of the "sociohistorical context" within which they exist.[71] He no less firmly rejects the ethno-particularism of both Afrikaans-medium universities and their black counterparts under apartheid. "In something close to a twenty-year period," he asserts, "the black universities have failed to produce a significant black leadership in the arts, science, medicine, politics, industry, and commerce. There has been no flowering of African scholarship either, and yet there are many substantive problems in our country today that require just this kind of informed leadership."[72]

Professor Manganyi accepts that South African universities may be said to be "under siege." In his view, however, this eliminates neither their duty nor their ability to devise "imaginative approaches" to the "Africanization" of higher education. He argues for "affirmative action" with the help of private finance in the training and subsequent hiring of black scholars and administrators at open universities. He argues for "faculty development" programs within South Africa to supplement "the annual trickle of African academics who study overseas under the auspices of such funding organizations as the Ford Foundation." He argues the need for all South African universities to play an active role in healing "the festering sore" of inadequate teacher training. He calls upon open universities in consultation with black community leadership to provide professional education for blacks in heretofore closed fields such as engineering,

71. N. Chabani Manganyi, *Mashangu's Revenge and Other Essays* (Johannesburg: Ravan Press, 1977), pp. 102–104.

72. N. Chabani Manganyi, *Looking Through the Keyhole* (Johannesburg: Ravan Press, 1981), p. 164.

architecture, business administration, and agriculture. Reflecting the changing perceptions of many black and a growing number of white intellectuals, Manganyi argues that South Africa needs appropriately Africanized universities.[73]

With African matriculants beginning to pour out of secondary schools, demand for university studies is on the verge of dramatic increase. Because bitter experience of apartheid has left them with special needs and concerns, African aspirants will care more about gaining access to education of quality and of cultural and community relevance than about whether they are to study alongside whites. They will be denied such access only at fateful social cost. Yet to accommodate them must mean to act swiftly to develop faculties and facilities and to finance educational programs at a host of duly Africanized universities. For South Africa, the challenge is imminent and portentous.

Modes of Education:
The Correspondence University and Technical Schools

Apart from residential universities, two other institutions play central roles in South African higher education: the correspondence university and the technikon. Issues of "open versus ethnic" and Africanization apply to them, too. But their development raises the additional question of the types of post-secondary education appropriate to South Africa's needs.

THE UNIVERSITY OF SOUTH AFRICA (UNISA)
With a faculty of 1,000, a student body of over 56,000, a huge administrative center and million-volume library in Pretoria, regional offices and libraries at Durban, Cape Town, Johannesburg, Pietersburg, and approximately seven hundred examination centers throughout the country, UNISA provides part-time university work by correspondence. Having begun with 1,248 students in 1948 and currently expanding at a rate of about 2,500 per year, UNISA plans to register over 100,000 stu-

73. Ibid., pp. 166–167.

dents by the year 2000.[74] Instruction is in both English and Afrikaans. It is racially open: about half of all the country's black university students are enrolled in UNISA.[75] It offers degrees ranging from bachelors to doctorates with 15 percent of its student body pursuing graduate work. Its Ph.D. recipients hold teaching positions at residential universities throughout Southern Africa.[76]

The faculty is predominantly Afrikaans, with a few African instructors in African languages and literature. Each faculty member is expected to spend a third of his time in research. Instruction covers the full spectrum of disciplines exclusive of medicine and engineering, though enrollments in laboratory sciences such as chemistry are limited by the need for students to have access to laboratory facilities in their locale or work place. Academic advising is done by mail and in person at regional centers. Course materials, assignments, study packets, books and examinations are sent through a computerized system at a rate of R190 for a regular (for degree students) three-course load.[77] Student performance is ultimately judged in three-hour final examinations at the end of the academic year (October–November).[78] The drop-out rate is about 50 percent the first year.[79] About 20 to 25 percent will complete bachelor's degrees within six to seven years.

74. For the official story of UNISA see Maurice Boucher, *Spes in Arduis: A History of the University of South Africa* (Pretoria: UNISA, 1973). UNISA publishes a monthly newspaper, *UNISA News-Nuus* (Pretoria: UNISA Department of Public Relations).

75. A UNISA brochure puts it this way: "Geographical and cultural obstacles are overcome without a need to bring students together on one campus."

76. According to UNISA Vice-Principal C. F. Crouse, two African faculty members of the University of Zululand completed UNISA Ph.D.s in 1981. Non-degree students make up about 10 percent of UNISA's enrollment.

77. The Ministry of Education and Training will refund this cost to African teachers. Similarly, corporations generally refund successful black students and deduct the cost from their business taxes as part of a national program to upgrade manpower skills.

78. A 4 percent upgrading factor is allowed for work assignments and can qualify a marginal student for a reexamination.

79. In a move that took excessively long-term degree aspirants off the rolls and resulted in a brief dip in enrollment growth, UNISA recently tightened enrollment regulations. If degree students fail to pass at least one (of three) courses their first year, they may enroll for a second year only if they

While UNISA is open to all communities and serves a growing black student body, it has not set for itself a special, urgent mission in black education. Scholarships (bursaries) are granted on a basis of merit, not need. Teacher training courses and a new research center on pedagogy and instructional technology (the Bureau for Teaching Development) are featured in UNISA literature without mention of distinctive needs, let alone a national crisis, in black education.[80] (Apart from UNISA, a considerable number of profitable, proprietary correspondence institutions operate in South Africa. Dr. Lawrence Keller of the USSALEP team estimates that they enroll from 75,000 to 100,000 persons, the majority of whom are black, live outside of urban areas, and seek pre–university level, career-oriented courses).

UNISA's School of Business Leadership does help upgrade the commercial and industrial skills of black small businessmen, but within a generalized, not specifically black-oriented context. While UNISA articulates a service mission for "the various communities in which it operates," and sponsors research in a wide spectrum of fields,[81] neither service nor research is consciously African-centered. It makes only modest gestures in the direction of the "sociohistorical" realities and needs about which black academics such as Professor Chabani Manganyi have expressed concern. Not only UNISA courses but UNISA public lectures, congresses, symposia, and cultural activities are open to the general public. And over time, the "general public" may come to include an increasing proportion of blacks. But major initiatives to adapt the UNISA curriculum, research foci, or staffing policies to meet particular needs of black communities

---

also take a prescribed bridging (remedial) course. Students must pass at least one course per year and complete their degree within a limit of ten years.

80. For example, the UNISA newsletter, *Progressio* 2, no. 3 (1980), describes the functions of a new Bureau of Teaching Development without any allusion to particular needs in black education.

81. UNISA research branches: Institutes—Labor Relations, Foreign and Comparative Law, Behavioural Sciences, Criminology, Continuing Education, Theological Research; Bureaus—Market Research, University Research, Teaching Development; Centers—Tax and Business Law, Agricultural Management Studies, Library and Information Services, Operational Research, Transport Economic Research, Management Studies, Sociological Research.

seem not to be contemplated. Courses in history and the social sciences suffer from the limitations of Eurocentric vision. All this said, UNISA, personified by its venerable and entrepreneurial Rector, Professor Theo van Wijk, combines a safe intellectual orthodoxy with an impressive and growing societal outreach and has become a significant force for the educational development of all South African communities.

TECHNIKONS

Government, business, and black community leaders commonly assert that South African education has been excessively theoretical and insufficiently pragmatic. The underdevelopment of training in applied sciences, technology, management, and allied fields has been decried by the National Manpower Commission, the de Lange Committee, and many educational critics. In the words of Kenneth Hartshorne, many persons now regard advanced technical education as being "more important" than "accelerated development of university education."[82]

Inspired by the technological achievements of Israel and Taiwan, the South African government has followed their example by instituting technikons. Even though technical and scientific training may be free from the questioning climate of a liberal education, and may therefore seem politically less threatening, the government applies apartheid to technikons as well as universities. Despite vacancies in white technikons, it is building separate African technikons in Pretoria, Umlazi (Durban), and elsewhere.

The USSALEP team visited a special technikon for Coloureds at Kasselsvlei near Cape Town. Under its Director, Franklin Sonn, the Peninsula Technikon is establishing itself as an aggressive educational force in the Coloured community.[83] Its 1,800 students learn business and industrial skills in a "hands on" fashion. Its mathematics faculty runs evening workshops

82. Hartshorne, "The Unfinished Business: Education for South Africa's Black People," p. 35.
83. See the Peninsula Technikon's representative description of the technikon approach to higher education in Document XVI.

for teachers. Its Deputy Director, Brian de Lacy Figaji, who gave up a promising career in private industry to serve his community, is organizing a program in applied engineering.[84]

All technikon programs and "diplomas" are organized parallel to but distinct from programs and "degrees" at universities. Diplomas range from a one-year certificate to a *laureatus* in technology equivalent to a Ph.D. Inevitably, technikon faculty, students, and diplomas face an uphill battle for recognition as being distinctive without being second-class. Ultimately, the ability of technikons to open doors to professional careers and to promote community development will determine their acceptance as institutions appropriate to the manpower needs of South Africa and to the socioeconomic needs of millions of undereducated, underskilled blacks.

Other Salient Issues

The USSALEP team found several sets of issues related to those of institutional appropriateness that confront South Africans with difficult choices.

AUTONOMY VERSUS STATE ADMINISTRATION

White universities as "autonomous" institutions are governed by university councils that include a minority of government appointees.[85] Block grants from the government make up about 75 percent of their operating budgets, the rest coming from student fees (20 percent) and private funds (5 percent). They

84. Figaji, who earned a B.Sc. at Western Cape, then a B.Sc. in Civil Engineering (with honors) at UCT, is intent upon developing courses that make a high-quality engineering program accessible to the Coloured community.

85. The University Council of Witwatersrand, for example, includes in addition to chief university administrators, eight members appointed by the central government, the Mayor of Johannesburg, four elected by convocation, five elected by the academic senate, three appointed by the regional Council of Education, two selected by alumni and donors, two each appointed by the City Council of Johannesburg and the Chamber of Mines, one each appointed by the Johannesburg Chamber of Commerce and Transvaal Chamber of Industries.

compete for additional capital funding from the Ministry of National Education.

Black institutions do not enjoy the autonomy afforded by funding channeled through relatively independent university councils. Instead, they are directly and fully government financed, putting them in what they view as second-class status. Their principals or rectors are not members of the prestigious Council of Universities composed of their white counterparts (and dominated by a 7 to 4 Afrikaner majority). Several, including the University of the North, Western Cape, Durban-Westville, and the Peninsula Technikon, have decided to seek increased policy flexibility and prestige by claiming an autonomy comparable to white universities'—at the risk of receiving less government funding. They are gambling, according to Peninsula's Franklin Sonn, that the government, because of manpower needs, will not financially penalize black institutions for choosing to exercise that measure of autonomy essential to academic quality. Black communities, of course, lack the wealth to make up for a reduction in government support by means of student fees and private contributions. Whether the government will in fact accord autonomy to black institutions without exacting a crippling financial price is to be seen.

ACADEMIC FREEDOM

Even the autonomous universities suffer from political constraints that seriously mar academic quality. Political informers infiltrate Student Representative Councils and classrooms. The government denies visas or passports to foreign and South African scholars at will, thus limiting international contact. It bans and restricts books. Rhetorical tracts of little intrinsic importance are its main targets, but the long lists of banned or restricted publications also include primary sources by historically important writers such as V. I. Lenin.[86]

Bent on increasing black enrollments, and seen as a center of liberal and even some radical thought, the University of Witwatersrand has aroused particular government ire. Indicative of

86. See Document XVII.

the costliness of giving political offense in the absence of a societal tradition of respect for Anglo-American values of academic freedom is the Transvaal government's recent invocation of political grounds in threatening to cancel a contract with Wits. Acting in the wake of a flag-burning incident on the campus, the regional government warned that the university was obligated to carry out a contract for teacher training in accordance with certain principles laid down in the Education Act of 1967. One of those is that children must be brought up in a Christian and national spirit and that teachers must be trained in this spirit. While a single incident was not held sufficient to warrant cancellation of the training agreement, the warning was ominous.[87]

Timidity, safe scholarship, and mediocrity are inevitable tendencies in such a climate of overt political pressure. In 1974, the status of their universities as internationally respected centers of learning and their collective integrity at stake, the Academic Freedom Committees of the Universities of Cape Town and Witwatersrand reviewed the concept and reality of academic freedom in South Africa. In a joint publication, *The Open Universities in South Africa and Academic Freedom, 1957–1974* (Cape Town: Juta, 1974), they significantly expanded their definition of academic freedom to include the "defense of social and personal freedom outside" as well as inside the university (p. viii). Their review concluded:

> The past fifteen years have seen the intensification of academic segregation and curtailment of individual liberty. The open universities have resisted these developments and endeavoured to preserve their standards and traditions in a society that has moved away from much of its Western heritage.
> The intensification of racial segregation in the universities has resulted in White and Black losing contact with each other. The universities have ceased to be the "laboratories of race relations"[1] that they are surely duty bound to be in a heterogeneous society. In the event all groups have suffered. The authors of *The Open Universities* expressed a simple truth when they declared in 1957: "The whole experience of eight centuries of university life makes it clear that the loss is not only to the excluded group, but also to

87. *Rand Daily Mail*, August 21, 1981.

those excluding them. Indeed the loss is to the whole community."[2]

As predicted by the authors of the 1957 work, "Black consciousness" has taken root on the Black campuses and contributed to the polarization of race groups in the university community and the wider South African society. Surely if the open universities had been permitted to continue their open-door policy much bitterness and friction might have been avoided. In the field of scholarship, too, the open universities could have made a more important contribution to South Africa. These opportunities have, however, been denied us and our society.

Unlike many institutions and much of the White population, the open universities have not remained mute while individual liberty in South Africa has been whittled away. They have protested loudly and vigorously in protest marches, picket protests, and public meetings and in deputations to the Government. Of course, there have been charges from time to time from the more radical members of the universities that these protests have not been strong enough. It may well be that impartial historians writing of our era a score or more years hence will conclude that more would have been achieved had no compromise been tolerated. The open universities do not claim to have a perfect record; they concede that survival as a liberal institution in South African society often demands compromises that they view as necessary in the circumstances but which may be seen by others as weakness. The record speaks for itself. The generations to come cannot but conclude that our open universities did not withdraw like the German universities in the 1930s, when Western values were destroyed.[3]

1. Professor P. V. Tobias, "The Cost of Academic Apartheid," in *Convocation Commentary* (University of the Witwatersrand) July, 1969, p. 16.

2. *The Open Universities in South Africa* (Johannesburg: Witwatersrand University Press, 1957), pp. 15–16.

3. In this respect it is important to recall the famous words of Thomas Mann in his letter to the Dean of the Philosophical Faculty of the University of Bonn, written in 1937, after he had been deprived of his honorary doctorate by that university: "The German universities share a heavy responsibility for all the present distresses which they called down upon their heads when they tragically misunderstood their historic hour and allowed their soil to nourish the ruthless forces which have devastated Germany morally, politically, and economically."

Afrikaner academics have traditionally seen the issue of academic freedom from a narrower perspective. To them it has meant the freedom to develop and safeguard a group's language and culture within its own academies. Thus they view academic freedom principally in collective, ethno-cultural rather than individual terms and are inclined to accept the need for conformity to certain *volk* values.[88]

"Despite all the restrictions that have been imposed there remains a considerable area of academic freedom in South Africa."[89] The accuracy of this assertion by the Academic Freedom Committees of the Universities of Cape Town and Witwatersrand is strikingly, often confusingly, evident to academic visitors. The following examples came to the attention of the USSALEP team. They probably reflect inconsistent policy more than an assured measure of freedom. But they are nonetheless interesting.

At the University of Cape Town, political science Professor David Welsh writes a monthly column for the Argus papers in which he typically asserts that government policy is condemning the society to "further polarization, more urban terrorism, . . . and a steady descent into a state of perpetual siege." At the University of Witwatersrand, psychologist Chabani Manganyi feels free to give (and publish) evidence in mitigation of sentence at a treason trial of black saboteurs, in which he analyzes the underlying social anomie and alienation that has led desperate young men to join the ranks of the African National Congress.[90] In the

88. See discussion in E. G. Malherbe, "Conflict and Progress in Education," pp. 179–183; David Welsh, "Some Political and Social Determinants of the Academic Environment," p. 27; and Johan C. Fick, "Afrikaner Student Politics—Past and Present," in Hendrik W. van der Merwe and David Welsh, eds., *Student Perspectives on South Africa* (Cape Town: David Philip, 1972), p. 76.

89. *The Open Universities in South Africa and Academic Freedom, 1957–1974*, p. 47.

90. Citing the destructive effect of rapid urbanization and government policy on African family life, Manganyi stresses the significance of an education-related generation gap within African society. "Usually the generational difference is not, as is often the case in more affluent communities, a matter of age. Here the difference is created at a more fundamental level by educational disparities between parents and offspring. It has become in most instances even a disparity in levels of political consciousness." Families are in a state of chronic financial and marital crisis. Traditional African values are assaulted by an "emerging ghetto culture." Alienated youth ideology is de-

pages of the official organ of the Teacher's League of South Africa, angry educators write of the "pigmentocracy" of an "overruled police state" and of "oppressed masses." The country's news media, one of the journal's authors has alleged, features "such a great deal of excited chatter" on the topic of "black education" that "newcomers to the South African scene might easily be deceived into thinking that they are witnessing a major event, nothing less than an educational renaissance. The truth is that 'black education' is as wretchedly black, as Stygian, as ever. The mock renaissance is just another ruling-class scheme to prolong the dark age into which their policies have plunged this country."[91]

The spirit of academic freedom doggedly persists. At the University of Witwatersrand the president of the faculty association, Professor Jennifer Thompson, reacted defiantly to government pressure stemming from student protests of June 1981. She announced that the faculty association intended to strengthen its ties with students, the Black University Workers Association, and the Administrative and Library Staff Association, for all had come to realize that they had a common aim— that of maintaining "our university as a body devoted to academic freedom." Together, she said, they would defeat "covert attempts to prove that a nonracial campus is doomed."[92]

ACCESS AND CURRICULUM

Blacks aspiring to higher education face formidable legal, financial, and academic hurdles and meet with varying degrees of help, hindrance, or indifference in trying to clear them.

---

veloping a "bond of secrecy" in the absence of effective adult guidance or educational experience. "The youth appear to believe as part of their ideology (their world view) that black adults are retreating from a frontal approach to South Africa's political problems. The legitimacy of such a verdict is not immediately at issue. What is essential for a dispassionate understanding of the situation is to know that the verdict exists." *The Voice* (Braamfontein), August 26, 1981 and September 6, 1981.

91. Joan Dalling, "A Lighter Shade of Black: The Undiminished Debasement of 'Black Education,' " *The Educational Journal* LII, no. 3 (Cape Town: 1980), p. 3.

92. *Rand Daily Mail*, August 31, 1981.

Blacks seeking government permission to enroll in open universities may now count on proactive support from the university administrations at Witwatersrand and Cape Town. Financially, however, they often need special help to attend Witwatersrand, where fees run between R500 and R1,080 not counting living and book expenses. It costs much less to attend a black university.

Wherever they enroll, black students find that the faculty and administration are mostly white. Piecemeal efforts are being made at open and black universities to train and upgrade black faculty. But until now at least, these efforts have not derived from systematic internal planning, intercampus cooperation or government initiative. In recent years, the Ford Foundation has sought to facilitate the development of black faculty in black universities by providing scholarships for graduate work in the United States. The prospect of major expansion in black higher education and the lack of qualified black educators underscores the urgency of this need.

As noted earlier, black secondary school students must contend with inadequate preparation and inflexible curricula. In addition to universities, several public service organizations are focusing on these problems.

The South African Institute of Race Relations (SAIRR) has mounted a variety of educational programs ranging from weekend classes for secondary school students (some taught by Wits university students) and workshops for black teachers, to bursaries and special tutorial programs for black university students. For example, in 1981 the Swiss government provided the SAIRR with R77,000 to administer a black bursaries project.[93] The recipients chosen include 40 part-time UNISA students (for whom SAIRR planned a careers workshop), 12 students at the University of Western Cape (where they receive special tutoring in study and language skills), and 15 students at various black and open universities (where individual mentoring is ar-

93. See F. C. Le Roux, "Report on Swiss Bursary Scheme and Enrichment Programmes at South African Universities and Sowetan Schools, 1981" (Johannesburg: SAIRR, March 1981).

ranged). The Swiss grant also covers a program of Saturday courses in language skills, English literature, science and mathematics, and career and self-exploration workshops for 65 preuniversity standard nine and ten Soweto pupils. To help close the gap in preparatory schooling, the German and Dutch governments, the Mobil Corporation, and the Genesis Foundation have made grants to the SAIRR and to the South African Council of Churches for similar initiatives.

Commenting on the overall need for university enrichment and bridging programs, the SAIRR maintains that an inferior educational system has left black secondary school graduates ill-prepared for university work. They face "insurmountable problems and thus the failure rate amongst the first-year students is alarmingly high—in some disciplines as high as 80 percent." At black universities the problem is "partially overcome by lowering standards"—an "inferior matriculation certificate" thus leads to an "inferior degree." At white universities most black students find it impossible to cope with the academic demands made on them and therefore require remedial work.[94]

The South African Council of Higher Education (SACHED), founded to counter the thrust of Bantu education, is concerned with both access and curricular issues.[95] With an emphasis on community-based undertakings, SACHED's "perspective is not that of assisting the underprivileged." It wishes, rather, "to provide resources which allow for independent self-help." Imperatives of economy and efficiency cause it to rely heavily on what it calls "distance learning systems," meaning the delivery of educational materials to people where they are. "A distance learning system also encourages students to become independent learners."[96]

94. Ibid., pp. 2–3.
95. The SACHED Board of Trustees as of December 1980: E. P. Bradlow, Bishop D. Tutu, Archbishop P. Buthelezi, Bishop M. Buthelezi, T. W. Kambule, G. R. Bozzoli, W. D. Wilson, T. Derkx, G. Pitje, E. Maurice, A. Moore, E. Mphahlele, A. Morphat, D. J. Cobbett.
96. SACHED Trust, *Annual Report 1980* (Johannesburg: 1981), p. 5. At the instance of Chief Gatsha Buthelezi, the Inkatha movement has founded its own KwaZulu Training Trust to foster a range of initiatives in community education.

In 1980–81 SACHED produced a five-volume, illustrated *African Studies Course*. Published and distributed through SACHED's affiliated Turret Correspondence College, the *African Studies Course* is written simply and with a clear conceptual focus. Exploring problems of causation, historical sources, interpretation, and bias, it prompts its secondary school–level readers to think critically. In 1980 SACHED's Johannesburg Center provided tutorials to 444 UNISA students (134 of whom were teachers) and cooperated with a U.S. International Communications Agency (ICA)/University of California–San Diego (UCSD) project to produce and test study materials for matriculation examinations, using local community tutors to extend their use. SACHED's Centers in Cape Town and Durban offer tutorial and basic skills programs of their own—though their efforts along with those of other organizations inevitably seem dwarfed by the magnitude of need.

The United States: Actions and Options

It may be hoped that the stark findings and urgent recommendations of the de Lange Committee report, *Education Provision in the RSA,* will force the pace of government and private sector action to meet the educational needs described in this report. Concurrently, it would be useful for Americans to ask themselves whether there is any way they might appropriately respond to the educational, and thus human, tragedy of South Africa.

Sizable numbers of South Africans study abroad (358 in Britain during 1978–79). But this does not reflect an educational dependency. South African institutions cover the full spectrum of scientific and technological learning and research. Though local educators complain that not enough students enroll in fields of national need such as mineral geology and mining engineering, such studies are available in South Africa—albeit essentially for whites.

Historically, American education has interacted principally with white South Africa. As of 1979–80 an estimated 1,170

South African students, including a small but growing number of blacks, were studying at universities in the United States.[97] American academia has also permanently attracted into its ranks some of South Africa's most able white scholars. Although they benefit from supportive interaction and colleagueship within national, essentially white, professional associations,[98] and from national research funding, English-speaking South African academics are most susceptible to external enticement. Some analysts attribute this to a lingering colonial sense of inferiority within South African academia coupled with "direct political pressures" and "gloomy political prognoses for the country as a whole." The result has been a significant "brain drain" of some of the country's "most talented scholars and students."[99] In August 1981, for example, Professor Julian Bienart left the University of Cape Town to become head of the School of Architecture and Planning at the Massachusetts Institute of Technology.[100]

Meant to infuse, not to drain, American educational programming for black South Africans is relatively recent. Such programming, the central focus of the USSALEP team's recommendations, has taken several forms. Since the early 1960s a U.S. government–funded Southern African Scholarship Program (SASP) for refugee students from the Southern Africa region has provided educational opportunities to several hundred black South Africans, some of whom are now teaching

97. The number doubled from 540 in 1975–76. South Africans were enrolled in a wide spectrum of fields: 16 percent social sciences, 14 percent business and management, 10 percent engineering, 8 percent in science and mathematics. See Institute of International Education, *Open Doors, 1979–80* and *Profiles: The Foreign Student in the United States* (New York: 1981).

98. For example, the Political Science Association of South Africa holds conferences and publishes a biennial journal, *Politikon*. There are no blacks on either the association's board of directors or the editorial advisory board of *Politikon*. In general, black membership in professional academic associations is minimal though not proscribed.

99. David Welsh, "Some Political and Social Determinants of the Academic Environment," pp. 25–26.

100. Dr. Beinart additionally became co-editor of the international journal *Space and Society. Rand Daily Mail*, August 31, 1981.

at universities or working as professionals in Lesotho, Zimbabwe, Zambia, and even South Africa, including Transkei.[101]

In 1979, the Institute of International Education (IIE) organized a South African Education Program jointly funded by American corporations, foundations, and universities. Seeking maximum impact and minimal discontinuity, the program offers graduate (mainly M.A. level) and advanced undergraduate training to black South Africans in the sciences, mathematics, economics, business management, and agriculture. Thirty-six students were placed in American institutions for the 1981–82 academic year. Screening of student applicants is done in South Africa under the guidance of an Educational Opportunities Council (with regional branches) and its director, Dr. Mokgethi B. G. Motlhabi.[102] For the 1981–82 academic year, there were also in the United States 19 new and 24 continuing graduate Fulbright students from South Africa, some of whom plan to resume or embark upon careers in black education on their return home. Additionally, the U.S. government's International Visitor Program brings white and black South African professionals to the United States for short exposure visits. And USSALEP arranges education-related exchange visits, as, for example, two recent tours of universities and research centers in the United States by multiracial teams of young South African academics.

101. Administered by the African American Institute (AAI) and the Phelps Stokes Fund, the SASP program has responded to the needs of young people whose aspirations for educational and sociopolitical change have brought them into conflict with their governments and caused them to leave their country.

102. Founding members of the Educational Opportunities Council: Bishop Desmond Tutu, General Secretary, South Africa Council of Churches (SACC); Dr. Ntbato Motlana, Physician, Soweto "Committee of Ten;" Leonard Mosala, Chloride Co.; Dr. Peter Hunter, University of Witwatersrand; Hazel Moolman, Assistant Director, SAIRR; Bernadette Mosala, SACC; Anne Rathebe, SACC; Michael Corke, Headmaster (private, multiracial) St. Barnabas College; W. Kambule, University of Witwatersrand; Winston Shuenyane, South Africa Breweries; John Samuel, Director, SACHED. A network of regional committees was established in 1981 in order to facilitate a broad national outreach and insure against the scholarship program being overly Soweto-centered.

In contemplating future action, Americans should be guided by concern for both principle and results. They should be motivated by (1) a desire to respond to the great thirst for education manifested by black South Africans; and (2) a realization that failure to respond would only favor prospects for intensified racial violence within, and East-West confrontation over, South Africa—developments that could undermine the racial cohesion and national security of the United States. Americans should act with the understanding that the peculiar circumstances of South Africa mean that any initiative worth taking will entail risk—of co-optation, rejection, or impotence. In human terms, however, they may reasonably hope that the application of a measure of "can do" resourcefulness to educational problems of South Africa could bring surprising results. With these considerations in mind, the USSALEP team proposes the following guidelines for American policy.

□ Americans should seek to promote racial equality in education. The thrust of their action should be to favor open access and improved quality of education at all levels for all communities. It should reflect an unwavering commitment to the principles of racial justice, meaning racial inclusiveness.

□ Americans should strive for maximal impact through projects with potential for multiplier effects, replicability, and/or validation. Every American-trained Ph.D. who returns to teach in an open or black university, every teacher of teachers who is equipped with new expertise on pedagogical skills, every workshop that improves the teaching of English, mathematics, or science, every book, film, computer, or study guide that is used and reused by motivated students and teachers, every catalytic act that brings white universities into positive collaboration with black universities—every one of these has the potential to ramify. Creation of a private technical school (PACE) in Soweto by American corporations, along with quiet negotiations for recognition of its unorthodox curriculum, embodies an appealing replicability. (On the other hand, it also suggests a danger that in the absence of black political authority, such initiatives may increasingly mold black education to the needs of private corporations.) Building training and testing components into programs such as UC San Diego's matric examination study guide project makes it possible to validate what works and what does not, and to correct, improve, or desist accordingly.

□ American initiatives should all respond to articulated community needs and be sanctioned by broad community support. They should be genuinely collaborative, free from paternalism and imposed ethnocentrism, which quietly stifle intellectual endeavor. They should be consciously aimed at a broad social spectrum, rural as well as urban, and sensitively avoid getting caught up in the imbroglio of competition or bickering among South African groups.

□ American projects should be designed to share knowledge, impart skills, spark creativity and foster self-reliance. This suggests the advisability of a diversity of projects and of an American role that is essentially short-term and catalytic.

□ American action should foster coordination and economy of effort. Educational efforts by foreign governments, corporations, and foundations are currently uncoordinated, fragmentary, sometimes redundant. Even private agencies within South Africa operate in substantial ignorance of each other's activities, thereby losing the potential benefit of shared experience and mutual support. To counter these examples of isolation and fragmentation that so plague South Africa, the following American endeavors would be appropriate: a comprehensive inventory of current educational projects and experience; a clearinghouse mechanism (preferably nongovernmental) to share such information on a continuing basis; and initiatives to promote cooperation among diverse South African universities, to encourage professional contact among teachers and researchers of all communities, and to extend educational projects (e.g., curricular and instructional workshops) across racial lines.

□ American public funds should flow through private American agencies to private South Africa agencies and should build upon local initiatives and structures. Relatively inflexible and compromising government to government interaction should be minimized in favor of cooperation with such groups as the South African Institute of Race Relations, SACHED, South African Council of Churches, the Council for Black Education and Research, the Urban Foundation, and universities, either singly or in consortia.

□ American actions should follow the dictates of strict cost-benefit analysis, leaving the South African government with full responsibility for funding its educational system. Pilot projects, distance learning, faculty exchanges, and academic workshops are examples of comparatively inexpensive modes of sharing knowledge and inspiring action. It should be possible to achieve important qualitative effects without assuming financial burdens that are properly those of South Africa.

Within the framework of these guidelines, the USSALEP team recommends a variety of endeavors. Specifically, it considers that an appropriate American response to the drama of South African education should include some or all of the following:

1. *Scholarship Programs.* Support is needed for a broadened range of scholarship programs for black South Africans. Continued support for a limited number of South African students obliged to flee their country for political reasons is justified. Dictates of economy and concern about "brain drain" suggest, however, that scholarships be offered for study at universities in Africa wherever possible. Critics of refugee education programs argue that they may serve to entice persons into exile. A way of minimizing this danger would be strictly to limit support to persons pressed into exile for other than educational reasons.

There should be expanded private and public assistance for the current IIE program. Focused as it is on graduate and advanced undergraduate students, it offers a liberating exposure to American culture and pedagogy. It avoids incurring the disorientation of prolonged absence and possible expatriation that would be risked by a four-year (plus possible graduate work) undergraduate program. Along with the Fulbright student program, IIE scholarships provide access to knowledge and experience that may help young blacks to assume leadership roles in education, business, industry, and public service. Also worthy of consideration: special scholarship programming in the key fields of teacher training and organizational management.

Given the importance of African-oriented education and cost-benefit budgeting, consideration should also be given to providing scholarships to black South Africans for study in neighboring African states. For example, the National University of Lesotho (NUL), which has set aside a 20 percent quota for foreign students, has indicated a willingness to enroll another 10 to 20 black South Africans. Eager to develop its own faculty and programs in such fields as health sciences, agriculture, and technology, a cooperative NUL would, in return, welcome Fulbright lecturers and opportunities to send instructors for advanced graduate work in the United States (possibly in exchange for hosting a group of American undergraduates on a year abroad).[103] Similar possibilities for Americans to catalyze programs of mutual benefit to South Africans and an African state host university might exist in Botswana and Swaziland, and conceivably farther afield in Zambia, Kenya, or even Nigeria. Another possibility to consider: the American University in Cairo (AUC). The priority of local needs rules out the University of Zimbabwe, which has in the past enrolled small numbers of black South Africans.[104]

Americans might also consider joining Swiss, Germans, and others in providing scholarships including tutorial assistance to black students at black or white South African universities. As Dr. Motlhabi of the Educational Opportunities Council has

103. Discussions with Vice-Chancellor A. M. Setsabi, Pro Vice-Chancellor L. B. J. Machobane and faculty at NUL.

104. Professor Walton R. Johnson of Rutgers University, on leave at the University of Zimbabwe, reported to the USSALEP team on his inquiries into possibilities for enrolling South African students in Zimbabwe. The question had been raised previously by the United Nations High Commissioner for Refugees (UNHCR). Dr. Johnson wrote: "In 1981, the university had 2,525 students. In 1982 it will have 1,000 new students. By 1983, enrollment will reach 5,000." Zimbabwe will be graduating 100,000 secondary students annually. Its university can only house 1,300 and is simply unable to accommodate students from outside the country.

commented: "It would be regrettable and ironic, indeed, if [white, English-medium] universities did not succeed in attracting and accommodating more black students . . . at this time when more U.S. universities are offering more admissions and scholarship funding to black South Africans." Dr. Motlhabi notes, however, that the obstacles to increasing such enrollments are less financial than those of securing government permission and arranging for suitable residences.[105] Finally, remedial programs at black universities badly need an infusion of ideas and support.

2. *Fulbright Lectureships.* Black universities such as those of Zululand, Transkei, and Bophuthatswana would welcome American Fulbright lecturers. The USSALEP team noted, in particular, an intense interest in the possibility of hosting black American scholars. The presence of these lecturers might do much for the quality of instruction and the self-esteem of host institutions. Fulbright lecturers might also bring fresh thought and vision to the classrooms of English- and Afrikaans-medium white universities. Opponents of such exchanges argue that they would imply endorsement of educational apartheid. Advocates respond that to persist in boycotting South African universities only leaves blacks further disadvantaged and isolated.

3. *Teacher Training.* The importance of teacher training has been cited repeatedly in this report. Institutions like Columbia Teachers College should consider joint ventures with universities such as Witwatersrand, Transkei, or Natal/Zululand and with organizations such as SACHED, SAIRR, or USSALEP, to organize special workshops in South Africa for instructors at teacher training colleges. (If this should not prove feasible, a select group of instructors and administrators from such institutions might be brought to the United States, albeit at greater expense, for intensive two- to three-month courses.) Additionally, Americans ought to consider helping to design and sponsor pilot workshops for upgrading secondary and primary teachers in South Africa.

---

105. IIE, South African Education Program. *Newsletter*, November 1981.

4. *TESL, Books, Instructional Technology, and "Distance Learning."* These options all deserve serious consideration. The United States could draw upon American educational experience and set up a program for Teaching English as a Second Language (TESL), possibly organized along the lines of the *Alliance Française*. A more ambitious, pace-setting possibility would be to incorporate such language training within a racially open American cultural center, replete with library and residential facilities, located near an open university. Americans could meet another important need by providing quality books, select journals, and video materials to desperately understocked black university libraries. Assisted experiments in computerized instruction (viz. the Plato project at the University of the Western Cape) might facilitate learning breakthroughs— and an American institution such as Indiana University might cooperate with a group like SACHED to develop a series of "distance courses" adapted to African conditions and needs such as UNISA is unlikely to offer.

Some suggestions to the USSALEP team on what Americans might appropriately do concerning South African higher education were very specific. For example, Professor C. van Onselen of Witwatersrand's oral history project would like to send black graduate students to the United States to work with distinguished scholars as apprentice researchers. Other ideas broached to the USSALEP team were contrastingly broad. Pertaining to such needs as the training of teachers, they would require much consultation with black and white South African educators to work out concepts and formats and would need at least passive South African government approval.

Existing programs on which new ones could be modeled have been cited in the body of this report—UCT's cadet scheme, Natal-Zululand inter-campus cooperation, UCSD's preparation of matric study guides, and various scholarship, distance learning, and upgrading projects. Cumulatively these undertakings should help to unleash a new, creative dynamic within South African education. As Americans explore ways in which they can most effectively contribute to this qualitative change, it will be essential to hold firm to principles of racial justice and to persuade black as well as white Americans that their actions can make a difference.

Americans also need to be realistic. Neither the dominant ideology nor the constitutional law of white-ruled South Africa is conducive to social and political reform. There is no chance that a *Brown* v. *Board of Education* case will crack the wall of apartheid surrounding South African education. Only a modest measure of hope is justified by the articulated goals of the de Lange Committee report and recent incremental gains in educational opportunity.[106] Nonetheless, it seems reasonable to assume that, over time, imaginative, catalytic initiatives in education might significantly further the cause of peaceful change. Respect for human dignity and intelligence dictates that Americans, eschewing self-righteousness and wishful illusions, act on this assumption.

106. Assistant Secretary of State Chester A. Crocker expressed a somewhat more optimistic view in a December 1981 statement on American policy and South African education. See Document XVIII.

Documents

Note on Sources and Editing

THE DOCUMENTS IN this section are based on materials gathered by the USSALEP team on their fact-finding mission. They have been abridged and in some instances—particularly in the case of talks not intended for written presentation—partially reorganized. Editorial interpolations and paraphrased materials are enclosed in brackets. Ellipses indicate major deletions. Numbered notes are part of the original documents, which are published here with the permission of their authors or publishers (except for materials in the public domain).

These documents represent a wide sampling of South African views, proposals, and programs with regard to educational change, as well as a proposed American response to the educational needs of black South Africans.

Soweto Schools Since the Riots of 1976:

An Address by Jill Oertel (1981)

The Soweto student riots of 1976 convinced the Department of Education and Training of the need to improve the quality and morale of the internationally visible Soweto schools. Under a voluble, pro-active regional director, Jaap Strydom, and within the bounds of Afrikaner-administered education for blacks, there were reforms. In the following address to an assembly of Soweto educators and corporate contributors (August 19, 1981), Jill Oertel, a leading liberal critic but also organizer of private-support for Soweto schools, describes educational reforms resulting from the cooperation of schools, the state bureaucracy, and private corporations and individuals.

The trauma of 1976 was a plea for change and brought about the virtual collapse of the black educational system. The [terrible] unrest called for drastic action, though no practical person claimed that the system could be put right overnight. [The] immediate need was for sympathy, understanding, and the courage to make fundamental change.

At the end of 1976, classes were empty and buildings destroyed. Teachers had lost confidence and children were hurt, bewildered, and filled with mistrust.

At least in Soweto much has been done to improve the situation, but I stress Soweto, for the same does not apply to other urban areas.

One of the first changes to be made was to place all secondary schools under the direct control of the new Department of Education and Training. It was generally agreed that the local school boards had lost control and the system could only be reorganised with a single controlling body.

To persuade the children to return to school was a more difficult task but by the end of 1978 thirty of Soweto's then forty-two high schools were almost full. In 1979 the high schools reopened with a total of 15,000 pupils. At this time many parents had sent their children away from Soweto, but as they regained confidence these children returned. Today there are 52,000 high school pupils and the problem is to keep outsiders from sneaking in.

Throughout the country, including the independent homelands, the increase in the number of black pupils has been dramatic. For example, in 1975 blacks at secondary schools constituted some 18 percent of all pupils; by 1980 this had risen to 58 percent. Against this background, expenditure on all education has remained virtually constant in real terms in recent years, [while] the disparity in expenditure between black and white has deteriorated further. Expenditure per capita is now of the order of R91 per black pupil compared with R740 per white child.

To provide the space required and to reduce class size, a massive brick-and-mortar programme was [begun] in 1978. Buildings were repaired, classrooms upgraded, additional classrooms built at existing schools, and thirteen new schools will have been completed by the end of this year. In my opinion the newest high schools are of a standard equal to high schools in the white areas. To date R21 million has been spent, but the programme is by no means complete.

There has also been a determined effort to upgrade teachers' qualifications, both through the In-Service Training Programme set up in terms of the Education and Training Act of

1978 and through Soweto's own In-Service Training Programme. In brief it means that all high school teachers have to attend training courses in their special subjects once a week. It is interesting to note that while the Department of Education and Training Programme is voluntary, the Soweto programme is compulsory, and 1982 has been set as the target date for all teachers to achieve their goals. In addition, teachers' salaries and conditions of service have been improved. These include parity of salaries at post 2 level, while ordinary teachers receive 75 percent of white salaries provided they have equal qualifications. Better service conditions include 100 percent housing loans and pension benefits. Finally, compulsory education has been introduced in two areas in Soweto and will be extended to other areas next year.

The growth rate to which I have referred placed incredible strains on our regional department and it is through their enthusiasm and determination that so much has been achieved. Certainly one must pay tribute to Mr. Strydom for his drive and energy. However, one must also pay special tribute to the private sector, service clubs, and individuals. Their support is actively encouraged by Mr. Strydom and they have shown their concern and willingness to assist. Undoubtedly their contribution has played a significant role in improving the quality of education.

It is worth mentioning some of the contributors [in] hopes that others will be encouraged to join this "special team." In 1978 the Anglo-American Corporation provided the financial backing for the Soweto Teachers' Training College. Moreover they have provided whole schools, both here and elsewhere. Fortunately they are not the only people to have contributed so generously. South African Breweries and Afrox have also donated whole schools and one must not forget the efforts of the *Star* newspaper.

Some months ago a group of leading companies which include Unilever, IBM, Dow Chemical, Ethnor, and Kodak launched the "Adopt-A-School" Project. These companies make contact with a school and then assist with teaching aids, school furniture, and building materials. I find the idea exciting because it provides a real opportunity for involvement—[beyond] simply writing out a cheque. Some of the companies have gone out of their way to get to know staff and pupils and to understand the [schools'] circumstances and priorities. Ethnor in particular have brought real love to their adopted school.

IBM have launched a R2.3 million video programme. The scheme consists of videotape instruction in the sciences and maths to senior schools. As a result more than 50,000 pupils will find maths and science easier and more exciting. Of the 5,400 pupils writing matric this year, only 1,930 have maths and 1,108 physical science as subjects. Although this is an improvement on 1979 when there were 899 matriculants, of which 210 wrote maths and 155 wrote physical science, the present numbers are far from satisfactory.

The PACE commercial high school is another significant contribution to Soweto. This is a private, fee-paying school funded by the American Chamber of Commerce and subject to inspection by the Department. The new school offers a wide range of commercial subjects and community involvement is placed high on its list of priorities.

The private sector rightly complains that black schools are not producing the people needed in the marketplace. Educationists and economists agree that there is an overemphasis on general academic values and that unless career education plays at least an equal role, pupils will continue to leave school with expectations completely out of line with [their employment] opportunities.

Mr. Strydom admits that the present ratio of fifty-five high schools to one technical high school is wrong. However, change must be relevant. A child must have a goal and the system must provide the opportunities for him to reach that goal.

The new plan for career education in Soweto is to be launched in 1982. It incorporates four streams—pure science, social science, technical, and commercial education. The streams are interchangeable and there is nothing to prevent a child changing course during the first three years of high school. At present ten high schools are being altered to provide for these additional courses. The conversion of one of these schools has been made possible through the support of S. A. Breweries. Specially selected teachers are being trained by the National Institute for Personnel Research to give vocational guidance classes.

Meaningful change and growth have been achieved in the past five years. A start has been made, and more important, a partnership has been established between the Department and the private sector to invest in and promote an educational system that will provide better training to fit pupils for the opportunities available.

However, much remains to be done. Unrest may flare up from time to time depending on the rate of progress and change. The authorities should recognise this danger and accelerate development.

But the government must go further. It is completely unrealistic to expect industrialists to assist in improving black education if there are no tax benefits. I know there are concessions for training workers but this does not solve the problem of training at the more formal level—and this is where the concessions for grants and loans should be. The government's cooperation with the private sector is vital if it is to be encouraged to play a full role. In his recent budget speech the Minister of Finance indicated that consideration is being given to allowances for educational contributions. It is sincerely hoped that such incentives will be [significant] and not long delayed.

Right now the task of educating the thousands of unskilled blacks falls willy-nilly into the hands of the private sector. To superimpose technical skills on pupils who have received a purely academic education must be one of the most expensive ways of training them. Furthermore such supplementary training will not adequately solve the problem of a pressing shortage of skills. In the long term, commercial and technical education at school level is clearly the answer, and is a far better solution than post school training by employers.

There are two ways of contributing [to continuing progress]—financial assistance and service. Both are equally important. The staff and pupils of black schools respond warmly to [outsiders'] interest. Furthermore, being involved [gives] one firsthand knowledge of [educational] circumstances and priorities.

When it comes to financial assistance, equipment for the new career-education schools is [a] top priority. Perhaps someone might be bold enough to provide a complete workshop.

[The Soweto project known as] R.E.A.D. provides a marvellous opportunity to be involved. [Initiated by the] chief librarian at St. John's College, it has researched and prepared lists of the most needed books, trained some sixty librarians, and raised more than a quarter of a million rands. Volunteers assist fifty-four libraries. Each school [needs] a full-time librarian. Perhaps someone would like to sponsor such a person?

Sport plays an integral part in our children's education but at present only five of Soweto's high schools have [even] limited facilities.

There are so many ways of assisting—some big and some small but all urgent. Imagine the ripple effect in other urban areas if we could establish the right standards in Soweto.

I was asked not to be too political today but [politics are unavoidable.] The present situation is of government making and its rectification is also a state responsibility. However, it is important to be realistic and to recognise that regrettably government lacks a sense of urgency. No one can deny it is in the interests of us all that dramatic progress be achieved in the shortest space of time. This is surely possible, if, instead of condemning past sins of omission or commission, we all recognise the challenge. A partnership of the public and private sectors can enhance the school system, giving more meaning to the lives of our young black people [while providing] the qualified manpower necessary to our economy. The Department is totally sincere in its endeavours to upgrade the system but needs our support to accelerate progress. Such support is surely one of the most rewarding ways of acknowledging social responsibility. As Jaap Strydom once said to me, "If you open the door, I will clinch the deal." I hope you will give him that opportunity.

A Report of the Education Commission of the South African Institute of Race Relations (1979)

In the aftermath of the Soweto unrest of 1976 in which general dissatisfaction with "black education" figured so prominently, the South African Institute of Race Relations appointed a commission to examine education in South Africa and to set out alternative policy guidelines for the country. Chaired by Professor G. R. Bozzoli, former principal of the University of Witwatersrand, the commission issued a report endorsed by the institute's executive committee in January 1979.

I. Principles

The Commission believes that a desirable educational system for South Africa should be based on the following principles:

1. There should be an emphasis upon equality of opportunity (for different geographical areas, sexes, social and ethnic groups), with supplementary allocation of resources for disadvantaged groups.

2. No form of separation of the various race and language groups into separate educational institutions should be laid

down in laws and regulations, and every effort should be made to integrate educational institutions at all levels.

3. The curriculum should stress not only the learning of basic linguistic, mathematical, and scientific concepts and skills, but also the stimulation of a critical scrutiny of society and encouragement in all pupils of an understanding and appreciation of the religions, music, art, literature, and history of other groups within South African society as well as their own.

4. A comprehensive programme of adult education in cultural, political, and vocational fields with particular attention being given to the establishment of functional literacy and numeracy programmes for all those adults who do not have these skills, should be embarked upon.

5. Education for the entire country should fall under a single ministry, and the system of educational decision-making and management should be designed to ensure effective participation of all interested parties at local and regional as well as national levels.

6. Independent (i.e. non-state) educational institutions, often centres of excellence and innovation, should be recognised, subject to state scrutiny in broad terms, to ensure basic compatibility with the spirit of society and the maintenance of acceptable educational standards.

The Commission considers these principles to be essential, and the following proposals for a new South African education system are based on them. It must be borne in mind that although it is not possible to predict future political developments in South Africa accurately, it seems likely that some form of consociational structure will evolve, possibly for a transitional period preceding the establishment of a unitary political system.

II. Proposals for a New South African Education System

1. DESEGREGATION

1.1 In principle there should be as little separation of ethnic and language groups as possible.

1.2 Initially many effectively separate institutions would persist because of current residential patterns. However it should be stipulated that where communities prefer culturally distinct schools or universities, access to such institutions should not be denied to members of other groups. It is the view of the Institute that the presence of members of other groups would constitute an enrichment rather than a threat to the dominant group attending the institution.

Since it is the aim of the proposed education system to ensure that institutions at the same level should be of a similar standard, it is unlikely that any institution would be swamped by an influx of members of another group. The United States' experience has shown that institutions tend to maintain their cultural identity when admission restrictions are removed.

1.3 Generally the highest institutions, i.e. universities, should be integrated first. Although ideally integration should commence at the earliest age possible, practically it would have to commence at university level. Some private schools would be among the first to desegregate, as they have already done to a limited extent.

2. CONTROL AND MANAGEMENT

2.1 There should be a high degree of decentralisation (on a geographical and not an ethnic basis) to provide for maximum involvement of the local community in education. All educational institutions (excluding self-governing tertiary institutions) in a particular regional unit should fall under the same authority, with due regard to the principle of participation and management set out in Principle 5 above.

2.2 Centralised control would, however, remain necessary in certain areas to monitor standards and ensure that the broad policy with regard to expenditure is followed.

  (a) Control of standards: there must be monitoring of educational standards at school level throughout the country by a small body set up for this purpose.

  (b) Inspectorate: an efficient inspectorate should, in addition to its normal functions, act to prevent regions from introducing ethnic or other forms of discrimination and to control regional spending in accordance with the principles of the national education policy.

2.3 The present National Education Council should be retained as a purely advisory body, but its sphere of concern should be extended to include the education provided for all people in South Africa. Its membership would thus have to be made representative of all population groups. The Council should regularly review the implementation of educational policy, and should report on this and recommend policy adaptations to the Minister.

3. ALLOCATION OF RESOURCES

3.1 Overall spending on education in South Africa is inadequate and the Commission recommends that public expenditure should rise from the present 4.33 percent to at least 8 percent of the country's GNP (noting that even this would be insufficient to equalise per capita expenditure on black and white pupils).

3.2 Allocation of resources should be such as to bring about a situation where education of an equally high standard would be offered to all groups at all schools and universities. This will demand major redistribution of resources.

3.3 The proportionate allocation of resources to education has undergone little change in the past twenty-five years. Without deliberate discrimination in favour of the disadvantaged there is likely to be little progress in equalising educational opportunity.

Certain groups and regions must be allocated extra financial resources which would serve not only to equalise facilities but also to provide for the payment of incentive bonuses for teachers assigned to special tasks.

Consideration should be given to the possibility of making a period of service in remote or deprived regions obligatory for all newly qualified teachers. Affirmative action would probably be an ongoing feature of the South African education system for the foreseeable future.

3.4 In order to decide how resources are to be redistributed, a means of assessing the standards and hence needs of educational institutions will have to be developed, as was done by the Karmel Commission in Australia. Such an assessment of present standards and future needs, based on the principle of equalising educational opportunity, could be carried out by a subcommittee of an enlarged National Education Council using the technical and administrative resources of the Human Sciences Research Council.

4. SPECIFIC EDUCATIONAL LEVELS

4.1 *Schools*

4.1.1 Curricula. The curriculum should reflect the multicultural nature of South African society. The drawing up of curricula and syllabuses should fall to a body of educationists including representatives of the teaching force and interested parties from outside the educational system.

Controversial social and environmental problems should be included in the curriculum, [as well as courses] dealing with the handling of inter- and intra-group relationships.

Provision must be made for affirmative action in the form of special courses for the disadvantaged.

4.1.2 Textbooks. Many current textbooks contain material offensive to certain South African population groups. Therefore existing textbooks must be reviewed and where necessary amended or replaced. Multicultural bodies should be responsible for the revision and selection of textbooks, which should be impartial and acceptable to all population groups.

4.1.3 Medium of Instruction. Recognising that at least for the foreseeable future it will be necessary for African pupils to switch from mother-tongue instruction to instruction in either English or Afrikaans, the Commission considers that there should be mother-tongue instruction in the early years of schooling, together with sufficient exposure from the beginning to the language of the parents' choice, which will later become the child's medium of instruction.

The nature of the transition from the mother tongue to another language as medium of instruction should not be rigidly prescribed. It should be possible for the child to become sufficiently proficient in the second tongue for the gradual changeover to have started by the third year of schooling, but this may be varied in accordance with the demands of the particular situation.

We also accept that the official language not chosen as medium of instruction should be offered as a school subject at both primary and secondary level.

4.2 *Universities*

4.2.1 All universities should fall under the same government department, and should be free to admit students and appoint staff, but shall not be free to exclude students on the grounds of race, language, or religion.

4.2.2 In view of the urgent need for rapid change in South African society it is imperative that universities, which should be closely involved in such change, should become primarily orientated towards the needs of South Africa, both in the training they offer and the research they undertake. The commitment of universities to a non-racial and more equitable South African society should manifest itself in a greater, more active involvement in the society.

4.2.3 Taking into account the vast educational inequalities which must be redressed if the number of black graduates is to be rapidly increased, universities will have to take positive action in a number of areas.

(a) Affirmative action must be applied in the selection of students. Although demonstrable academic potential remains a basic criterion in such selection, it should not be seen as sole and sufficient reason in itself for admission.

In the case of academic staff, academic achievement is the basic criterion for appointment, but it should be borne in mind that if curricula are to be orientated towards local needs, in some areas the best qualified persons for certain posts would be black, and universities should take positive action to train persons to fill such posts.

An additional criterion of selection should be commitment to an active involvement in South Africa.

(b) Universities must provide appropriate educational services for adults, particularly blacks, wishing to do part-time degrees by means other than correspondence study.

(c) Universities should take an active part in the provision of programmes to upgrade the qualifications of black teachers and hence the quality of education for blacks, this being essential if the number of black matriculants and black graduates is to be increased significantly.

4.3 *Intermediate Qualifications*

The importance of intermediate qualifications, particularly in the technological field, must be stressed. People who compose "middle level manpower"—including the technician in industry, the medical aide, the dental aide and responsible health personnel, the draughtsman, the survey technician, and other paraprofessional persons—are in very great demand. Yet while they are highly skilled, educated, and trained, they do not require the breadth of expansive university education essential for fully professional people.

Polytechnic institutions of good quality are needed to provide this essential kind of person, and in the absence of special polytechnics, the Colleges of Advanced Technical Education could be used. The universities should play an important role by diverting students with the appropriate attributes to these institutions, and by taking an interest in and even participating in their training.

4.4 *Adult Education*

4.4.1 The inability of the various education systems in South Africa, and particularly those for blacks, to cope with all the needs of the country and its people makes adult education [a] high priority, [which] might even warrant the diversion of resources from the school system.

4.4.2 Adult education should be based on the premise that education is an ongoing, lifelong process. But it is likely that in South Africa, a developing country, vocational [training and basic education will be stressed.] [Adult] education should [encompass]

(a) "Upgrading" education. Probably the most important area at present, this would include functional literacy programmes, part-time school education programmes for adults compelled to drop out of school at an early stage, and in-service training programmes for workers, including teachers.

(b) Adult education in the more general sense, which would be aimed at the cultural enrichment of the individual and society and which could include education related to the needs of the individual and the community.

DOCUMENT III:

Identity, Culture, and Curriculum:

Lectures by H. J. Coetzee, N.C. Manganyi, and M. C. O'Dowd (1978)

The Senate of the University of Witwatersrand presents an annual series of lectures devoted to matters of great concern to the public which it serves. In September 1978 the topic was "South Africa's Crisis in education." The following lectures—by an Afrikaner anthropologist, a black psychologist, and a manager of the Anglo-American Corporation—were among the most challenging of the series. All take as their point of departure the curricular issues raised by the problem of identity in culturally diverse South Africa.

IDENTITY, CULTURE, AND CURRICULUM (I)
H. J. COETZEE. Professor of Social Anthropology,
Potchefstroom University for Christian Higher Education

As an anthropologist and an Afrikaner, I assume that the term *identity* refers to cultural and ethnic identity.

The Oxford Dictionary defines *identity* as the quality or condition of being the same; it means absolute or essential sameness; the concept expresses a feeling of oneness.

The concept positively relates to a group consciousness; to a particular awareness of ethnic and cultural sameness; of being one with others having the same awareness. It suggests a psychological state of being bound up with others. At the same time a value consciousness, a need for belonging, and hence an aspect of personal security are essential ingredients of the state of identity.

In a world of sociological, cultural, and religious diversity, of mutually complementary or opposing, inclusive or exclusive groups, a single person can identify with a vast number of groups. The more composite the social milieu, the more complicated the bonds of identification are sure to be. In a so-called primitive and relatively small society, the groups or units constituting the band, clan, or tribe are arranged and fixed by custom and tradition in a more or less harmonious and generally accepted way. A male, for example, identifies with males, a single male with the single male group, the uninitiated with the boys, etc., in the smaller relevant units. The same with females. But males, as a group constituted by all [sub-groups] of males, [distinguish themselves] from women in their constituent groups. However, males and females identify with the same inclusive group. As a group they may identify with another "related" group but not with a "foreign" group. On this level "foreign" is usually coterminous with "hostile," and "stranger" with "enemy."

The general web of identifications sets a smooth course for interpersonal behaviour, and provides an atmosphere of security right through all layers and sectors of the small-scale traditional society.

On this level of society identity is mainly, if not exclusively, prescribed. The members are not confused by personal choice and decision, [and hence are] subjected to few strains or tensions. The members of the group as such share the same religion, the same overall values, taboos, tastes, etc. Education is focused on a perpetuation and maintenance of exactly these values and customs, the existing way of life. The members may even be unconscious of their identity. What is, was and shall be.

Shirokogoroff rightly draws attention to the phenomenon that (ethnic, cultural) self-consciousness results from contact with and hence consciousness of "foreign" ethnic/cultural units. Identification with its resulting security might be the cause of opposition to change and of deep emotional tension accompanying cultural adaptation, which is in itself a process of change, demanding new identifications. A new religion introduced into a once mono-religious society demands a choice of religious identity; it brings about the existence of a new group; it asks for a new arrangement of identity relations; it increases the complexity and creates differentiation in various sectors of everyday life: marriage (polygamy vs. monogamy); mores (sexual practices); economy (war, hunting, and cattle rustling as economic pursuits); clothing; sacrifices; a rearrangement of constitutive groups and identifications—if they can be harmonized.

It is not difficult to [imagine] the general psychological and personal confusion of a person [who] all of a sudden finds himself confronted by a multitude of diverse cultures differ[ing] in civilisation, norms, behaviour patterns, religious values, language, [and] status. [Differences that could be regarded as] mutually complementary easily [come to be] regarded as competitive or exclusive. Confusion and uncertainty of identity tend to disintegrate both group and individual.

Culture

A South African audience need not be lectured on the reality of cultural multiplicity. [But the opposing tendencies of government policy and settlement patterns have produced a uniquely problematic relationship between geography and ethnic identity in South Africa.] Neither the remnants of traditional ethnic and cultural settlement patterns, nor the most rigorous government efforts to maintain [the] cultural homogeneity [of geographic areas], could prevent large-scale contact, penetration, and settlement of [diverse] cultures within the same spatial borders. The historic background of the relations between cultural groups [is also] relevant. A past fraught with enmity and conflict leaves a heritage of suspicion and fear. . . .

[Under these circumstances], rigid uniformity [of] curricula [is] easily regarded as unjust[ly] limit[ing] the liberties and rights [of] ethnic, religious, and cultural [groups]. However, general human, cultural, and civilizational features constitute a reality as potent as individual, group, and cultural diversity. It belongs to the essential functions of education to develop *human* potential, to stimulate and enrich culture, to promote civilization, to prepare the younger (human) generation to move to adulthood and to train them to earn a livelihood. . . .

Taken as a whole, curricula ought to stress both the common or universal and differentials such as cultural, ethnic, linguistic, and religious identity—[emphasizing] diversity in harmony (unity) and unity with diversity rather than either diversity or unity for its own sake. The leading principle to be followed [is] that education has to observe both the particular and the universal as basic realities of life. . . . This demands an educational system with central control over standards, organisation, and basic curricula, but simultaneously decentralised according to the demands of the basic group identities.

IDENTITY, CULTURE, AND CURRICULUM (II)

N. C. MANGANYI. Research Fellow,
African Studies Institute, University of Witwatersrand

[Culture, Symbolisation, Identity, Heroes]

Culture is a medium for human self-extension and transcendence. As symbolisation, ritual, [and] intersubjectivity [by means] of which shared meanings and significances are attributed to a shared universe, culture [constitutes] notions of individual and group identity.

When the going is good, concern about culture and identity is conspicuous by its absence. When the chips are down individuals as well as nations become introverted like the textbook adolescent because they require an inner sense of direction. A preoccupation with identity during moments of crisis in a life history and in history are of significant diagnostic value. This introversion and preoccupation with distinctiveness are not in any way spurious. Individuals or groups whose identit[ies are] well articulated must necessarily lose some of [their] appreciation of the value of others since [their] distinctiveness thrives on exclusion. One does oneself a good turn and dehumanizes someone else in the process. . . .

In the beginning was the word. The word was *written* and *spoken* and it was, as blacks know so well, about God and whiteness, the devil and blackness. This, apart from the violent wars of conquest, is the fundamental statement which needs to be made about the interface between blacks and whites in the eighteenth century and beyond. It was the power of the word, the power of language, the tyranny of the symbolic which introduced psychosocial dominance of the blacks by the whites. It was culture developing negatively.

In the beginning of the cultural interface there were guns and assegais, Bibles, English readers, and culturally distinctive rituals. There were ideals which supported specific cultural idioms and identities. Indigenous marital negotiations and respect for ancestors found [themselves] on the defensive during that period.

Confronted with a strange land, a new human landscape, the culture of the gun and prayer was on the offensive and it braced itself accordingly to conquer and convert the indigenous peoples.

In any society, social and cultural institutions are a materialisation of the primacy of subjectivity—the achievement in practical terms of man's capacity for symbolisation. Institutions retain their symbolic power and meaning primarily because they clarify for a society its own cultural identity to the exclusion of other societies.

Although white South Africa *cannot* strictly speaking be said to have developed a national culture that is homogenous, it has, however, developed a geopolitical and race-supremacist identity spearheaded by Afrikaner *volk-nasionalisme*. The unhealthy aspects of this identity and nationalism arise from its preoccupation with the exclusion of the country's black majority.

The white geopolitical identity with its exclusive cultural idiom is successful insofar as it can assert itself in terms of its military power, its economic and technological advances, the visibility of its secular shrines, and the (diminishing) power of its psycho-social dominance of blacks. What we blacks absorb from this culture are not white South African cultural specifics but universals from imperialistic cultures such as that of the United States. The local varia[nt] of Western culture is soured for us by its intransigent preoccupation with exclusion and self-preservation.

Perhaps one lesson here is that [the attempt] to legislate culture and identity [produces] stasis and sterility. If we put legal constraints on our interpretations and the meanings we attach to certain cross-cultural and racial transactions, we make culture hostage to purely political designs which enshrine naked power at the expense of humane government and good order.

Once culture begins to thrive in the bosom of a defensive nationalism, [it] loses its power to creatively transform society. [It] becomes a survival culture and thus fails to generate new meanings and symbols for people to cherish. Very often a survival culture has its origins in protest. In the case of black culture, protest [is] inspir[ed by] the people's innermost concerns. Needless to say a protest culture such as we have in the major urban black centres is also in important psychological respects a survival kit. It also suffers from too shameless a preoccupation with certainty and the need for the elimination of ambiguity. It would be a serious cultural tragedy if this protest culture should lose touch with traditional African cultural forms. It should continue to enrich itself from this source in its specific idiom. On the other hand, some strands of the current urban black culture are absorbed from the black experience, notably in the United States and post-colonial Africa.

Repudiation—that almost happened to us. We were for a time in our history as black people on the verge of caving in—spiritually, culturally, and psychologically—to the tyranny of the symbolic, the sheer power of psychosocial domination. Through education and Christianisation we were almost seduced into self-negation and other forms of mindlessness.

Culture can consolidate group cohesion and national identity without suffocating the concurrent blossoming of individualised identities. Culture can expand human consciousness, yet when it develops negatively as has been the case in South Africa it becomes an instrument for the subjugation of the human spirit. Man's capacity for symbolisation expresses itself in various ways. On the positive side, we can identify the capacity for the development of language, ritual, as well as such products as art and technology. On the negative side we [can] witness this gift lead[ing] to atrocious excesses and the development of powerful fantasies of racial superiority. Language, for example, can be an important instrument of liberation, and yet it quite often becomes an instrument of oppression. In our history, those amongst us blacks who became alienated from their Africanness and blackness did so in some respects because they became absorbed into a new language idiom—a new way of experiencing, thinking, and doing. . . .

[South Africa's] past is unclear because our history of black-white conflict, dating back to the earliest black-white encounters, has left us a legacy of heroes that we are unable to identify with and share across cultural lines. The English in South Africa have their Cecil John Rhodeses, the Afrikaners their Piet Retiefs, and we blacks our Shakas and Langalibaleles. The poverty of our national cultural life is [evident in] the absence of heroes whose esteem in national life transcends racial, ethnic, and cultural boundaries. The partisan heroes of the past will not do for the future of this country and its peoples. The new heroes will consist of those of our people who without regard to questions of colour will assist the country out of the grips of the encapsulated siege cultures of Afrikanerdom and black consciousness.

Africanisation [is] an invigorating belief system [with much to contribute] in the sphere of national and cultural identity. I see [it] as the main dynamic force in cultural terms which can move the country beyond the present cultural stàsis. Even black consciousness and Afrikaner *volk-nasionalisme* must not be allowed to atrophy before they have made possible the creative synthesis which must certainly occur, unless the national consciousness is handicapped by a "repetition compulsion" to take to arms at the end of each century.

Needed: A New Language for New Meanings

The state of culture and identity in South Africa is such that there is no language free of partisan interests to communicate the new meanings which await South Africans in the future.

The reference here is not to the cluttered imagery of political discourse, nor even is it to the bloated metaphors that are created by patriotic sentiment. I am referring to the potential language—the potential cross-cultural and inter-racial conversations which should be going on in the consciousness of creative artists and opinion makers [and should be providing] meanings and symbols [for a new] collective national culture. Culture is metaphor and it is, perhaps, language in its most pregnant and complex form. When we write, paint, sing, and dance primarily to conserve culture we kill something—the communication, clarification, and elaboration of new meanings and insights. We impoverish [rather than] develop and consolidate culture and identity this way.

Culture as metaphor, as language, as communication, flourishes only in a climate of freedom—in a climate within which paradoxically individual identity is cherished more than collective or group identity. This issue of individual identity—the freedom to be—is closely associated with the question of censorship which, in our case at least, is [the] handmaiden of our conservationist approach to culture and identity.

Our situation demands that we examine dispassionately the extent to which the limitations arising from censorship diminish our sensibility as a people as well as the prospects for change. Before any political solution (however peaceful it may turn out to be) is brought to bear on the problems of this country there is going to be a great amount of anguish. One day we will all have to learn to be free, to be members of a natural community and not a community of victims, and that in itself will be painful. It is time we allowed ourselves a foretaste of this pain. Therapeutic doses of [it] must be sought in the freedom and individuality (identity) of our artists, writers, and academics.

In our situation this individuality of the artist or writer is held hostage not only by legal censorship but perhaps more importantly by self-censorship. If self-censorship were completely conscious—if each one of us as it were held a hearing in which the pros and cons of an idea were logically debated—[self-censorship would not be] so disturbing. The danger [is] that a great deal of this selectivity occurs at a preconscious level and it is here and yonder where the most fertile image and ideas come into being.

Calls for "education for an African future" must be thoughtfully extended to include education for freedom and equality. For whether we like it or not post-colonial Africa will have to realise these values more and more in the future. The hodgepodge that is education in our country today is not futuristic enough. It is so intimately tied up with our outmoded ideas about race and our conservationist approach to culture and identity that it hardly is a preparation for the kind of Southern Africa that is emerging on the historical horizon. Education should always be futuristic. It is anticipatory even in the case of the individual child or student. It concerns itself with realities and potentials in the individual which are activated in anticipation of future participation in society.

Anticipation of the future requires an appreciation of the present and past. It is my view that in South African academic life today there is little which approximates this searching appreciation of the past and present. For example, it may well be that much of our history is in need of serious reinterpretation. Most of what occurs in the spheres of economic, political, and cultural life also require[s] analysis and research. Is it not true that most of the writing and teaching on African literature written in English is undertaken beyond our borders? What of serious work in such relevant areas as inter-group conflict and conflict resolution?

Our failure as academics and students to grapple with substantive problems, to develop a pedagogy and analysis that is pragmatic as well as relevant for freedom, equality and an African future is illustrated [by the fact that] within universities debate on the critical issues facing South Africa [is] too often blunted, or even avoided. Particularly contentious or sensitive areas of the society are often only marginally examined where they are examined at all. "In political science it is the exception rather than the rule that any detailed or empirical analysis of the South African political system is presented in the classroom. In economics such sensitive topics as income and wealth distribution, trade union and labour relations and patterns of corporate ownership and control are all but avoided, in part because so little research has been conducted in these areas. . . . In psychology no deep study of the psychology of race and racism is offered by any South African University."[1]

In my own speciality, psychology, training and study programmes need to reflect concern with the significant problems of individuals and groups in this decidedly African context. What we have [instead]—and we must thank the Anglo-Saxon world for it—is a *bourgeois psychology* concerned mainly with such profit and loss issues as production and motivation, particularly of blacks. Psychologists who have the intellectual grace to leave [such topics] alone will not [abandon] that other favourite pseudospecies of psychology—the white rat. . . .

IDENTITY, CULTURE, AND CURRICULUM (III)
M. C. O'DOWD. Manager, Anglo-American Corporation

In his address, Professor Coetzee pointed out that education in the modern world has a dual function—to help develop the individual as a human being and to provide [him] with technology. The question of cultural identity is relevant only to the first of these objectives [because] technology is [universal]. . . . [As Pro-

1. David Welsh and Michael Savage, "The University in Divided Societies: The Case of South Africa," in H. W. van der Merwe and David Welsh, eds., *The Future of the University in Southern Africa* (Cape Town: David Philip, 1977), pp. 144–145.

fessor Coetzee also pointed out], we live in a world in which the individual's identity [as] defined [by] group membership is very complex indeed, because he is a member of many groups that overlap with each other and that may either reinforce or conflict with each other. . . .

In discussing [the] question of identity, it is important to recognize that although one is talking of identity in terms of memberships [in] groups, it is individuals, not groups, who have identities. As the Austrian economist Von Mises points out in his great work *Of Human Action*, in all human affairs only the individual acts. So if the individual identifies himself with a group, it is the individual who is identifying himself; if the individual says that his membership [in] the group is more important to him than his individuality, it is still the individual who says so; if the individual believes that the group is more real than he is, it is still the individual who believes it. The practical implication of this is that the individual can leave the group and the group can be destroyed by the defection of its members without any of its members being destroyed in the process. This is the difference between a group and an organism. Your hand cannot defect from you without dying, but a human individual, or for that matter an animal, can defect if circumstances allow.

This fact creates one of the great paradoxes of group identity. To the extent that the individual identifies himself in terms of his membership [in] a group, it is extremely important to him that other people should continue to identify themselves with that group. If all the other members defect, the group has ceased to exist, and the last individual, who does not defect voluntarily, has been deprived of something which was very valuable to him. This gives rise to the historical tendency for individuals to attempt to coerce other individuals in terms of group membership, in order to preserve the groups which are important to them. So the importance of group membership to the identity of the individual has been and still is the major source of the violation of the identity of the individual, leading others to force on them membership [in] groups with which they do not identify, or to force them to remain members of groups which they wish to leave.

This is not to say of course that group identity is unreal; indeed, if it was unreal the problem would not arise. Those who have been the victims of the form of coercion to which I have referred often seek to promote a solution based on the abolition of groups and group identities, but I think we have to admit that, even if this were desirable, it would be a vain hope. Group identities are a major fact of life and their existence has to be accepted. At the same time it is an equally major fact of modern life that group identities are never simple, and those who hope to eliminate the complexities of their life by seeking a completely mutually reinforcing set of group identities are doomed to disappointment. . . .

We need to give some special attention to the concept of nationality. Most of us have been more or less brought up to believe that nationality is the governing group identity; that it is more real, more fundamental, and more far reaching than any other; that, above all identities, the individual has a "national identity." Yet when we look into history, we find that this belief is of very recent origin, and we also find that for all the emotion associated with the concept of nationality, it is quite difficult to find out what it means. As a matter of legal reality, nationality means legal subjection to a particular government, or, more accurately, a particular sovereign government. But this hardly ever enters into the discussion, since nationality is used to legitimate the sovereignty of governments, so that one is in danger of getting involved in an entirely circular concept.

There was, particularly in the 19th century, what one could call a Platonic idea of a nation [as] a group of people with a common language, a common religion, a strong emotional sense of identity, and who were the citizens and the only citizens of an independent sovereign state. But when we look in the world for an embodiment of this Platonic idea, we cannot find one—not even one. When the idea was at its height, France and Britain were commonly held up as the models, but neither fits the bill. In France there is a Breton-speaking minority and a Basque-speaking minority; in Britain there is a Welsh-speaking minority and a Gaelic-speaking minority. In neither case is their language the monopoly of their citizens. There are French speakers in Belgium, Switzerland, and Canada, and English speakers all over the world. They do not have a common religion and only to a limited extent a common history. In terms of history is Britain a nation or are England and Scotland nations? Scotland is a particularly interesting case. Many Scots say that Scotland is a nation yet Scotland has two languages, and the language of the majority is English. Scotland has a longer history as part of Great Britain than as a unified kingdom of Scotland. The highlands of Scotland have been ruled from London for much longer than they were ever ruled from Edinburgh, because, in the days of the kingdom of Scotland, the kings in Edinburgh only effectively ruled in the Highlands from time to time, and never for very long. Yet many Scots feel that Scotland is a nation.

In fact, when one looks into it, the concept of nationality, which has been so loudly proclaimed [as] the most fundamental of man's group identities, is a very dubious one. It has a long history, but in the form in which it was taught to us it was actually invented in the 19th century, for the specific ulterior motive of justifying the putting together by violence under one government of everybody who spoke German, except those who happened to be too strong to be subjected to this treatment. There was no reason why the German-speaking people of Bavaria should be unified with Prussia while the German-speaking people of Switzerland and Austria should be left out, [aside from] the facts of power at the time. Bavaria had as long and respectable a history as a separate entity as Austria had, and actually, [in terms] of ethnicity, the people of Austria, Switzerland, Wurtemberg-Baden and Alsace are one people in a way that the Bavarians and Prussians are not.

We must also recognize that because the 19th-century version of nationality did not represent the recognition of a reality, but an attempt to impose a theory, it gave rise to a great many evils. In theory the nation had a common language, so language minorities were an anomaly which had if possible to be made to disappear.

Those who have read *How Green Was My Valley* will remember the concerted attack which was made on the Welsh language in the state's school system in liberal 19th-century England. For the purpose of creating the desired degree of homogeneity in the national state these policies failed. The cultural identities which were persecuted not only survived but in a certain way flourished, but this does not mean that these policies did no harm. The situation of having to fight for survival against persecution makes a culture unduly backward-looking, conservative, encapsulated; deprived both of much of its creativity and of its ability to coexist creatively with other cultures.

When we come to South Africa, and ask what nation or nations are there, it is difficult to escape the conclusion that there are none. To say that all the inhabitants of South African territory or all the subjects of the South African government constitute one South African nation is to fly in the face of the declared views of many, but not all, of the people concerned. On the other hand, to call various linguistic or ethnic groups within South Africa "nations" seems to be stretching the term even further than it has been stretched by others. One or two of the groups, notably the Afrikaner and the Zulus, seem to have many but not all of the traditional characteristics, but with most of the rest of the population it is not even clear into what groups it falls. In the last resort it would seem that nationality is subjective. A group of people are a nation who believe they are a nation, but we have the complication in South Africa that the beliefs do not correspond with the groupings to which these beliefs apply. We have the kind of situation where A says that his nation consists of A and B and C but B says that he is a nation on his own and C that his nation consists of everybody from A to Z. Even [in] a subjective theory this produces no nation, for A, B, and C can only constitute a nation if A, B, and C all agree that they constitute one.

The significance of all this when we come to the preservation or recognition of identity is that we have to acknowledge that identity can be preserved but cannot be created, and that the identities which have to be preserved or respected [must] be real, that is to say identities with which large numbers of people actually do identify. It seems to me that there can be no solution to this problem in a society as complex as South Africa, except

on a basis of voluntarism. There has to be room for people to
create institutions based on various group identities—not only
language but also religion and culture, and people have to be
free to identify with these as they prefer.

Now this proposal is not simply a cunning trick to bring about
a melting pot and the disappearance of group identities. There
are cases which illustrate that separate identities can survive side
by side without any overt coercion for centuries. A case in point
is Lebanon where there are four communities based on language and religion, two Christian and two Moslem, which have
coexisted for over a thousand years. Whatever the position may
have been in the distant past, for many years now the schools of
each community have been open to the children of the other
communities and in most schools a small minority will be found
of children of all three of the other communities; yet there has
been no evidence that any community has made significant
headway in assimilating any of the others.

Of course Lebanon has got into very serious trouble in recent
times and one hesitates to hold it up as a model, but this trouble
had far more to do with the Arab-Israeli war than with any
breakdown of the system of inter-communal relationships, and
whether or not the constitution of Lebanon was satisfactory, the
experience certainly shows that different communities can coexist in the same country without coercive beaconing off. In
South Africa separate groups do exist, and to the extent that
these groups wish to perpetuate themselves they must be allowed to do so. Any attempt to subvert them will be counter-
productive and very damaging. At the same time the groups in
question must be real: they must exist in the minds of their members and not only in the minds of other people. And it is neither
necessary nor desirable that there should be coercive drawing
of the lines between them. In terms of the drawing up of curricula at school level, what is required is both more diversity than
we have at present and more voluntarism, indeed, a situation
more like that which exists among the universities in South Africa but going further than it does there at present.

Of course, this applies only to the curricula in cultural subjects. Going back to Professor Coetzee's original division, in the

technological subjects there is no room for cultural diversity. There is no English mathematics, Afrikaans mathematics, or Zulu mathematics—mathematics is mathematics.

That concludes my main theme, but I would like to lend support to Professor Manganyi's plea that we Africanise our education, particularly at the university level. In the main, this means that we make our education more relevant, not [only in] cultural but [also in] technological subjects. Mathematics is mathematics, but it is appropriate that when we apply it to engineering problems we should apply it to the type of problem which arises in South Africa, and the same is even more pressingly true in the social sciences. To take an example with which I am personally connected, the criticism used to be raised in connection with the Wits School of Social Work that it was training social workers to work in America, that when they graduated they knew what the social problems were in Chicago and how to handle them but they had no idea what the social problems were in Johannesburg. Now I am glad to say that this is being corrected. Vigorous and effective measures are being taken to ensure that the social work students are trained to do social work on the Witwatersrand.

I cannot help thinking that we need to attend to the same problem in areas like sociology and economics. Part of the trouble stems from the inevitable predominance of American textbooks, but there is also the desire among academics to keep up with the Joneses in the academic field by writing about the things which people in America are writing about. This, I would suggest, is self-defeating. No sociologist sitting in South Africa can possibly make a real contribution to the understanding of social problems in Chicago, but he may well be able to make a study of social conditions in South Africa which will interest even people in Chicago. In the social sciences, research has to be about something. It cannot be done in the abstract, and the only social problems which South African sociologists can possibly research are the social problems of South Africa. This means, of course, that not only must they research South African social problems, but in structuring their undergraduate syllabuses they must equip their undergraduates to research South African social problems. Our law faculties have never had any difficulty about teaching South African law nor our history faculties about teaching South African history. Why should our sociology and economics faculties have difficulty about teaching South African economics and sociology?

In conclusion, as one of them, I would like to [address] English-speaking South Africans. The great fault of English-speaking South Africans, as I see it, is that they do not have sufficient respect for the cultures of other people. In general they have maintained an open culture which anybody is free to join who wishes, and this is a very good thing to do, but it is not a substitute for having proper respect for the cultures of other people who do not wish to join. The English culture is a very fine one but it is not, as its holders are all too inclined to assume, superior to all others in all respects, and still less is it the be-all and end-all, containing so much within itself that nobody need look outside it. My plea is therefore that the English-medium universities specifically should not only ensure that their curricula are fully relevant to South African problems but also that their curricula are rooted in an adequate respect for the cultures of other people and in particular of the other people who live in South Africa.

We have to Africanise the subject matter of our curricula, but we have also to Africanise our thinking and our basic attitudes, and this will have to flow in due course into the schools.

One of the positive implications of this is that [where] we have sought to preserve our cultural identity by deliberately or inadvertently fostering hostility to other cultures, we will have to stop doing this. Indeed all groups in South Africa urgently need to stop this practice.

No culture [that] is worth anything needs to foster hostility to others in order to survive, and in any case as we live and have to live in the same country this is a practice which we simply cannot afford.

The Council for Black Education and Research (1979, 1981)

Led by Professor Es'kia Mphahlele, the internationally re-spected novelist and essayist and Senior Research Fellow at the African Studies Institute, University of Witwatersrand, thirty-three black educators met in February 1981 at the Central Methodist Church of Durban and agreed to create a Council for Black Education and Research. Presented here are (1) an abbreviated text of the original proposal (dated August 1979) to create the council and (2) a selection of diverse, representa-tive statements made by participants at the 1981 Durban con-ference.

1. Text of Original Proposal

[OUR CURRENT SITUATION]

Education has become a subject of the gravest concern among Blacks in South Africa since June 1976. Many recommenda-tions have been made by people from a variety of organizations for the resolution of our educational problems. In many cases recommendations have been made without a proper grasp of the facts concerning education in South Africa. We know that the most sensitive area is in Black education, where the problems are innumerable. Black students are doubly handicapped: not only do they receive a poor education, but they are ignorant about organizations and foundations that can assist them in the effort to improve and further their studies. We as African educators and educationists have not made ourselves heard loud and expertly enough to serve as a resource for positive enlightened opinion on educational matters. Our teachers, like our doctors, lawyers, nurses, social workers, businessmen, and representatives of other professions, have for several generations been engaged in the sheer effort of survival. Thus we have tended to think of ourselves as trade unions, each in our respective career. Even here our gains have been minimal, given the tight sociopolitical structures we work in.

We have for several generations been a subject for research among White scholars who have invariably discovered in us a mine willing to be excavated and to yield treasures of information. White scholars, driven by the impulse of adventure and desire to know, have exploited their privileged [position] to explore new areas of knowledge. This is only human. They have, however, neglected to take us along with them; even as apprentices, alas, as they opened avenues of exploration in the natural, physical, and social sciences, and in the humanities. They have produced textbooks which we have to study at school and university. Some of the texts have been elevating and informative; others have been tinged with a sense of superiority, or even with racism. All the same they examine us on their own textbooks and supervise our dissertations for senior university degrees. They continue to monitor our intellect and our emotional responses.

Black creators of imaginative literature have documented the drama of African life. Within the constraints of the censored imagination they have served as historians of feeling who make us aware of ourselves as we are, have been, and as we aspire to be. Apart from these, apart from one single mathematician whose work is a school text, and apart from scattered articles on subjects relating to the social sciences, where do we as Africans stand in scholarship? Nowhere. Our closeness to physical pain in the social and physical conditions in which we are compelled to live; and survival: these have been our major concerns as writers. Even the literature we produce is the spontaneous cry of the tortured soul, a more excruciatingly compulsive act of self-expression than it is for our White counterparts. And yet, meaningful literature should [enlarge] the reader['s sensibilities] and strive to take him beyond the pain, the predicament, of the present. Not towards a bloody revolution or simplistic resolution of our plight, but towards a humanistic self-esteem, to an awareness of the larger human environment.

Because we are nowhere in the landscape of scholarship except as a subject of study, we can never challenge untruths and half-truths or critically examine statements White scholars make about us. Our gut responses alone simply will not do. We lose by default, by not being there where the debate rages, in the halls of learning. Not even our authorities on African languages are teaching us anything new through the printed word. Only Black South African expatriates like Dr. Daniel Kunene (Sotho, Zulu, Xhosa), the late Dr. A. C. Jordan (Xhosa), and Dr. A. Moloisi (Sotho) have been active in this field. But then their voices reach us from the United States. Yes, our efforts have been preempted. True enough, it is only in the last decade that publishers have become more sympathetic with and more solicitous of our literary enterprise and are ready to print what we can write. True, also, our education has not in the past twenty-five years encouraged independent thinking and research. Yes, we have been survivalists. But we alone can generate the intellectual energy to outlive our present conditions.

THE SELF

This requires that we generate enthusiasm for scholarship among ourselves and the energy to realize the goals we have set ourselves. Although we have adopted certain Western values, some of them uncritically, there is still a solid irreducible core of

traditional humanism in us, given the separateness of our existence in South Africa. And our humanism has been open to some
very positive Western influences, e.g., education before 1953,
social organization, democracy as a concept, societies that prac-
tise it, and so on. We need positive scholarship to continue the
road to self-knowledge, to functional self-awareness. The self
needs to be liberated; this is only possible when it develops
through an all-round education.

THE COMMUNITY

This is another level into which we as intellectuals should move.
For this, we need a machinery that will translate our research
into community projects. Although there is still a solid core of
traditional idioms in the way we dramatize our joys, our sorrows,
and other emotions, and our aspirations common to all our ethnic enclaves, we need *direction*. Educational planning based on a
sound, workable philosophy is imperative. Such a philosophy
must needs seek to unify the sensibilities of our urban and rural
communities, whatever boundaries are drawn for us. This is
where education becomes a tangible vehicle of culture, and
helps us seek and find a point of reconciliation between the humanistic, liberated self and the technological environment that
industry creates.

Implied in a philosophy is a myth. A myth determines a point
of view. A myth also implies that options must be identified. If
we can crystallize into a slogan for education the belief in liberation of the self and relevance to the community, [in accord with]
our humanistic traditions rooted in social relationships and
compassion—if we hold dear these ideals, and never let them
out of sight—our educational planning will have a purpose. For
too long we have had to "educate" for other people's purposes
which in turn derive from Eurocentric principles of education.
Even while we have to do the bidding of the authority that plans
for us, *we* ought to be able to evaluate what we are commanded
to do and know not only what we could do if we had a free hand,
but also how we can inject a new sense of purpose into the existing conditions.

At the community level we need to think and plan up and down the vertical scale of achievement and along the horizontal plane of schooling for the largest number. We need to think of education from the preschool level through secondary and tertiary levels; we need to think of technical and adult education. We should also be thinking of commercial or business training that can be conducted on a short-term diploma basis to produce bookkeepers, typists, personnel managers, school counsellors and school social workers who can be attached to school districts. Career guidance must become an indispensable feature of our school systems. We should move away from the assumption that everybody wants, or needs, or is mentally equipped to manage, an arts or science degree; we should move away from the notion that "woodwork," handicrafts, the fine arts, are for the dullards and so make them an organic part of the curriculum; gardening should cease to be [a punishment] for pupils. We should be bold enough to envisage a system that will produce diploma-carrying graduates in the areas suggested above who can create their own jobs in a community and need not always be employed by someone else. Career guidance expertise will need to be enlisted right at the beginning, even before we can produce our own. But such initial expertise should be informed by knowledge of our cultural background. We have also to include the plastic, graphic, and performing arts in our planning, so as to avoid wastage of human resources and so that education be a process of spiritual self-fulfillment as well as preparedness for economic well-being. A division of English studies is most necessary to help students and working people to cope with their learning and career obligations.

Another concern is the quality of teaching. Teacher upgrading requires an intensive programme that will also make it possible for us to follow up on in-service training, so that our teachers can be assisted in putting their knowledge and skills to good account in the field. This means that in-service training should be a continuous process, allowing batches of teachers to return to it time after time. Academic upgrading and methodology should go hand in hand.

THE MACHINERY

In order to address the above problems, [we propose the establishment of a] Council for Black Education and Research. Such a body should comprise a select group of teachers and educationists who will seriously apply their minds to the promotion of its aims as spelled out above. The Council must have a strong African base. The service of right-thinking expertise sympathetic to our cause will then be solicited from among White educationists for specific projects. Such personnel should at the same time be prepared to assist in the training of Black researchers. White researchers should be prepared to be briefed by the Council's executive authority and to ask the questions we want answered in the [course] of their work. . . .

AIMS AND OBJECTS [OF THE COUNCIL]

1. To collect information concerning education in South Africa and such other countries of the world as may be relevant;

2. To assemble and evaluate existing educational theories and practices in South Africa;

3. To disseminate the information among such persons and organizations as we may consider to have the potential of furthering the aims of the Council;

4. To conduct research into other areas of Black education including available resources for student aid, statistics regarding students' and teachers' needs, schooling facilities, the financing of Black education, manpower in both urban and rural areas, curricula, and so on;

5. To evaluate existing textbooks and prescribed books;

6. To initiate programmes for informal education, seminars for teacher upgrading, and any institution the Council may deem necessary and feasible for furthering the education of African people; to work towards the establishment of a multiple-stream institution for long and short training courses;

7. To establish a centre where reference books and documentation will be housed and made accessible to Blacks who want to do educational research; to provide a library and reading room in such a centre;

8. To raise funds to finance the Council's projects.

[COUNCIL PROJECTS]

1. The upgrading of teachers in Mathematics, English and the Sciences.

2. Informal educational programmes, preferably interdisciplinary within a seminar and/or workshop framework. Academic support and enrichment programmes for students and teachers who cannot cope with higher studies.

3. Evaluation of curricula and syllabuses.

4. Evaluation of school texts—handbooks and prescribed literature in various languages. We have the right to lead in the choice of texts.

5. A career-guidance service.

6. Adult education [for] parents as learners, and as mothers and fathers of children in school, at teacher-training institutions, and at university.

2. *Statements*

□ "Black" has [no] cultural reference. It is only a convenient political term. We should prefer to be called "African" when we want to be culturally distinguished. Whites have never identified with African culture and its beliefs, thus they remain Europeans. "Black" in the context of the Council name refers to all those who are not officially designated "white." We need, however, to do research into African culture to arrive at an enlightened redefinition of ourselves. "African" is a term we can live with till eternity, because long after a greater nonracial South Africa has been attained, we shall still be *African*, belonging in spirit and in fact on the continent of Africa. We should strive towards a point where we can determine our cultural choices. In a future South Africa, there will be a majority culture, i.e. the culture evolved by the majority of people who have attained the status of self-determination as a nonracial society.

□ The process of creating our own culture is not simply an educational one but also a political one. We have to get away from concepts like "black," "coloured," "Indian" in South Africa and come up with such a concept as "Azania." No oppressor can now identify with the concept of "Azania." "Azania," like Namibia, is a concept with which only a people struggling for liberation can identify. What we need is a "Council for Azanian Education and Research."

□ There has been no significant scholarship coming out of the black universities. The job of academics is not only to teach or publish, but also to research problems that affect the community.

□ Religion was used by the colonial administrations as an instrument to dominate the African. Study of religion is one way of decolonizing the mind. We should restore indigenous religion as a basis of self-discovery. The Christian churches themselves can also assist in the process of decolonization.

□ We should not get bogged down in the idea that we cannot educate effectively before the existing political system falls away. There is still room for manoeuvre in community education. We are dealing with communities that have not been pushed to think seriously about African culture, such a concept being almost foreign to their struggle for survival.

□ Research requires techniques, and we should consider how we are going to prepare people for reseach. We do not have researchers among Africans, because our people have not been trained. We find ourselves relying on whites who are trained. Universities could be good training ground if they were institutions that expressed *us* as a disadvantaged people.

□ Arising from the suggestion that we enlist the support of the teachers and the parents are the questions:

(a) what [do] we do in the case where teachers refuse to be involved in educational efforts off the schoolgrounds?

(b) how do we deal with the present situation where the parents' right to participate in the education of the black child has been preempted by the state?

□ We would like the ideas we express here to reach the teachers as the living link between makers and critics of policy and the children. We have to grapple with the problem of reaching the teachers. We need to adopt a more positive attitude towards them rather than treat them as an inferior and reactionary species, because we could close [their] minds to anything progressive by our own attitude towards them. Even if we wanted to work through the teachers' association it [would] not [be] easy to get through to the teachers. There is no difficulty with the few politically conscious and progressive [ones]. But the greater mass do not attend meetings, conferences, seminars. We should [however] use every opportunity to address teachers' meetings where educational strategies are being discussed, so as to join in the more enlightened teachers' efforts to bring others into our orbit. We should also try to use the press as an instrument of communication among ourselves, as a vehicle of ideas. The teachers are themselves victims of a system. Not many of them have been under the kind of teacher who inspires the right attitude to history and a higher self-esteem. For every such teacher there [are many who are less fortunate, as well as] students who spy and inform on him or her.

□ The events of 1976–77 exploded the myth [held by] teachers that students were lethargic and uncritical in class: another indication [of] the teacher's need to reexamine himself and his educational principles and practice.

□ The teacher's integrity and self-respect are at stake when it comes to teaching "sensitive" subjects like history, geography, literature. Should he reinterpret texts in such a way as to correct a racial bias that demeans the black man, even if it should mean that the students will fail in the public examination for replaying his interpretation? Teachers at all levels are faced with this dilemma.

□ Those of us who had the advantage of coming into contact with progressive systems of education in other parts of Africa and elsewhere abroad have a duty to perform: to cogently argue a case for such alternatives as they propose, and to write down their ideas and disseminate them.

□ It would be unrealistic of us to think that we can put our ideas into practice within the existing structures of our society, much as we are agreed that the curricula and syllabuses designed for us need overhauling. A way of realizing some of our ideals would seem to be through interdisciplinary adult education. This is a community programme and is the least problematic area. Newly independent countries like Tanzania place a premium on adult education, because, as President [Julius] Nyerere says, the educated adult can make an impact *now*, whereas the student at school has still a long way to go before his relevance in the community can be felt.

□ The Council should begin to explore the Africanization of our curricula. The educational system designed for us, indeed like the one designed for whites, is an extension of Western structures. Africa is not the first frame of reference in this structure. From primary to university schooling Western theories form the basis of approach to the disciplines we teach. For instance, little is being done to establish psychological theory based on the Africans' indigenous thought and belief. The industrial psychologist asks questions about the African working class that have little or nothing to do with the deeper levels of the indigenous experience, [or with] traditional African thought and belief. Our children may know European and American history and never get to know the local history of their own people, of their subcontinent and of Africa at large. Africanization should be [conceived] as a process of decolonizing the mind.

The de Lange Committee Report on Education in South Africa (1981)

In June 1980 the South African government commissioned the independent but state-funded Human Sciences Research Council (HSRC) to carry out a comprehensive review of all levels of South African education. The HSRC chose Professor J. P. de Lange, the Rector of Rand Afrikaans University, to serve as chair of a distinguished steering committee of twenty-seven members, including several leaders in black education (e.g., A. C. Nkabinde, Principal, The University of Zululand; F. A. Sonn, Director, Penninsula Technikon; and R. E. van der Ross, Principal, University of the Western Cape). De Lange organized a massive research effort and a year after its creation the steering committee submitted a unanimous report to the government. The fifth and final chapter of the report proposed "A Programme to Attain Education of Equal Quality For All Inhabitants." The abridged text follows.

Introduction

The meaning of education of equal quality and the manner in which it should be achieved have received much attention during the past decade or two. Only limited success has been attained in introduc[ing] such education in different parts of the world.

The limited success can mainly be ascribed to bias, incorrect premises, and overestimat[ing] the [importance] of, for example, symbolic measures.

An attempt has been made to learn from experience in this regard. What follows is an exposition of

□ Premises
□ A short evaluation of the present educational system [with] equal quality as a criterion
□ Problems in formulati[ng] operational criteria relevant to education of equal quality
□ Proposed policy guidelines
□ Implications of these guidelines
□ Priority recommendations

Premises

The pursuit of equality basically involves the desire to adhere to a particular social-ethical concept regarding the structure of society, namely that the right of every individual to receive equal treatment in the allocation of collective benefits in the social structure should be recognized and guaranteed. This goal is not based on an assumption of sameness or uniformity between people. It does however postulate a common humanity and the right every person has to expect that organized society will acknowledge the intrinsic values of individuality and humanity and promote the realization of these values.

The demand for equality in education is of special relevance as a result of the restriction of available resources and when the real danger exists that as a consequence of the existing obstruction persons or groups may be denied their rightful share in the benefits that education offers. The term "rightful share" cannot be interpreted as an "equal share" in the arithmetical sense of the word, since no society can function on the basis of unqualified equality. . . . "Rightful share" should therefore be understood as being related to the concept "distributive justice." The demand for equal share in education is only viable as a principle of distributive justice—"equality-in-the-light-of-justice."

"Rightful distribution" in the first place demands that the rules of distribution be formulated and applied in an unprejudiced manner and, secondly, that the demand for fairness should be met.

Since distribution rules in themselves can be unjust, even if they are applied in an unprejudiced manner, the demand for justice with regard to distribution rules implies that in the rules there should be no discrimination between people unless *relevant differences* can be indicated, necessitating differentiation. The principle of "equality-in-the-light-of-justice" therefore does make provision for differentiation in the distribution rules and for this reason "rightful share" does not merely mean "the same share for everybody." Equal education therefore does not imply identical education for everybody.

The main problem in determining what a fair share is, lies in the differences between people that could be raised as conditions for distributive differentiation and consequently for categorizing. Justice demands that such differences should be *relevant* differences, i.e., they should relate to the benefit that will be considered for distribution. . . . The operational criteria for the application of the principle of equality (in the sense of "for each and everybody his rightful share") should therefore be related to the character and meaning of education.

A further problem is to determine what should be regarded as the "character and meaning of education." This question is basically concerned with the mutual relation between the education curriculum and those matters that are regarded as important by society. Which aims should be served by institutionalized education?

The answer probably lies in the balance between the following community values:

1. *Formative religious education,* i.e., to give the person taught an opportunity to experience formative religious education in accordance with his own convictions.

2. *The maintenance and elaboration of cultural values,* i.e., to equip the educational client (sometimes the learner, sometimes the parent, sometimes the community) with an appreciation of cultural heritage as well as with the critical and creative abilities essential for cultural renewal, taking into full consideration the requirements of the different cultural groups; and to give them a share in the control of the contents of the curriculum for the members of the cultural group concerned.

3. *Raising the material standards of living,* i.e., to equip the educational client with the necessary skills to be economically productive in accordance with his individual potential, as part of the trained and active labour force; also to enable him to meet his individual needs as well as the collective needs of society.

4. *The development of innovative and adaptive abilities with regard to the demands of cultural change,* i.e., to equip the recipient of education with knowledge and understanding of the requirements of continual cultural change, for example how to adjust to new situations, to cultivate a productivity-oriented ethic of work, and to master new technological knowledge and skills.

5. *The improvement of interpersonal relationships,* i.e., to equip the educational client with knowledge, interaction skills, and a sense of social responsibility which can promote mutual respect, trust, and cooperation between individuals and groups.

6. *The cultivation of positive civil attitudes,* i.e., to equip educational clients with knowledge regarding the history, geography, fauna and flora, system of government, etc. of the country, as well as with the problems and challenges facing society.

7. *The promotion of the overall quality of life,* i.e., to give the educational client the opportunity to develop as a complete, responsible individual: for example the cultivation of language, arithmetic, and manual skills; the cultivation of the ability to learn and evaluate independently; the cultivation of a personal system of values; the identification and development of the largest

possible variety of individual talents; the improvement of physical and mental health; the cultivation of specialized professional skills as well as social and leadership skills.

Evaluation of the Present Educational Dispensation in South Africa

In the existing provision of education, differentiation occurs in different ways and on different grounds between educational clients. The same advantages are not available to everyone.

Some of the grounds on which differentiation occurs, for example ability, interest, aptitude, and occupational orientation, are probably relevant and consequently meet the demand for justice insofar as they have a bearing on the nature and meaning of education and its requirements as a social practice.

However, differentiation also rests purely on the basis of race or colour, which cannot be regarded as relevant for inequality of treatment. Examples of this are the treatment of different racial groups in a way that is strikingly unequal, for example in the distribution of education in terms of *per capita* expenditure, proportion of qualified teachers, quality and quantity of facilities such as buildings, equipment, and sports facilities. A further example is where admission to educational institutions is regulated mainly on a racial basis. The result is that an individual, owing to his being a member of a particular racial group, does not or cannot receive his rightful share in the provision of education. Differentiation based purely on differences of race or colour, [which] cannot be regarded as relevant grounds for inequality of treatment, is contrary to the social and ethical demands for justice.

If provision has to be made for a programme of education of the same quality for all population groups, the distribution of education will have to be organized in such a way that everyone will receive a rightful share, regardless of race, colour, socioeconomic context, ethnic context, religion, sex, or geographical location.

Problems Connected with the Formulation of Operational Criteria
with Regard to the Concept "Equal Quality in Education"

The approach to the concept "equal quality in education" can be narrowed down to two points of view: that of *educational achievements* and that of *educational opportunities*.

The interpretation of "equal quality in education" in terms of achievement refers to the level of education or proficiency attained by the educational client attributable to educational activities. This interpretation creates several problems. To ensure that every individual attains the same level of achievement, all possible factors which may prevent equality of the end result, e.g., differences in aptitude, mental abilities, and ambition, will have to be eliminated. The implications of such an ideal will be a programme of levelling which cannot be implemented and which in any case is ethically unacceptable.

The interpretation of "equal quality in education" in terms of *opportunities* means that everybody, regardless of race, colour, language, socioeconomic status, faith, or sex, is given the same opportunities to obtain a fair share in the benefits that education offers. However, this interpretation also creates several practical problems if the educational system is expected to give all educational clients an equal opportunity to exercise their claim to education as a social benefit. These problems are revealed in a clear definition of what is meant by "equal opportunities" and in the determination of where this same "starting line" is, with due allowance for factors that may cause an unfair advantage or disadvantage for some participants. Attention will have to be paid to matters such as the socioeconomic position of the individual's family and other environmental factors which influence his school readiness and learning ability. Attention will also have to be paid to the position of the community of which the individual is a member, for example the extent of its effective participation in decision-making with regard to policy issues such as the allocation of resources, the determination of priorities, and its executive function. For the rest, attention will have to be paid to the question of *admission* to available educational institutions, for example the range of choices, the degree of freedom of choice, the geographical distribution of school facilities, the extent of compulsory education, compulsory schooling, and "free" instruction, the quality of available educational facilities. Absolutely equal opportunities can be achieved only if all impediments in as well as outside the school are eliminated. Owing to the many causes of inequalities outside the school, little success has been achieved to date in creating equal educational opportunities in both developed and less developed countries.

Because of the extremely complex problems standing in the way of a positive definition of "a programme for equal quality in education for all population groups," an answer could perhaps [be] found [by adopting] the following as a point of departure: *the reduction and elimination of demonstrable inequality in the provision of education available to members of the different population groups.* Such inequalities can be clearly defined and documented as concrete, empirically determinable facts on the basis of several specific indicators:

1. Accessibility, including freedom of choice in the sense of the absence of educationally irrelevant limitations.

2. Curriculum content and standards, for example subject choice, syllabuses, textbooks, evaluation criteria, examination standards, certification, and general administration.

3. General compulsory education, for example a specific number of years agreed upon.

4. Teachers, for example level of training, teacher-pupil ratio, etc.

5. Physical educational facilities, for example the number and quality of buildings, equipment, sports facilities, etc.

6. Financial resources, for example per capita expenditure.

Proposed Policy Guidelines

1. The progressive provision of adequate means to enable every inhabitant to obtain the essential minimum of knowledge,

skills, and values will be recognized and maintained as the highest priority in the programme for the provision of education.

2. No person will on educationally irrelevant grounds be debarred from available educational opportunities from which he might benefit.

3. In the formal organization of the education system in respect of matters such as buildings and equipment, pupil/teacher ratios and the qualifications of teaching staff, the provision of equal advantages for all pupils and students of a particular educationally relevant group will be recognized and maintained as a priority.

4. Where educationally irrelevant inequalities are indicated in the provision of education, educational reforms in the interests of justice will be aimed at the elimination of such inequalities.

Implications

The above guidelines are collectively aimed at establishing a new educational dispensation to promote the progressive implementation of the principle of education of equal quality for the different population groups. This does not mean that on a given date the education system will be reformed to such an extent that "equal quality education" will immediately be provided in an *absolute sense*. It is unrealistic to expect that such an objective can suddenly be achieved. The achievement of this general *objective* can nevertheless be systematically striven for through the achievement of definite *aims* and the determination of clear *priorities* in terms of specific action programmes.

The first guideline implies that provision should be made for the introduction of *general compulsory education and compulsory schooling linked with "free" education* for a certain number of years. It is self-evident that the pace at which compulsory schooling can be progressively extended will depend mainly on the availability of manpower and funds. The guideline implies, however, that [increasing the extent and duration of] compulsory education should receive the highest priority.

The *second guideline* [implies the need for] clarity on the *methods and pace* [of] eliminat[ing] *restrictions on access to and the provision of* educational facilities based purely on racial or colour discrimination. *Methods* [include] the use of statutory, organizational, financial, and other arguments, while *pace* [refers] to the phasing of measures to ensure an appropriate transitional and adjustment period. This guideline does not mean that the provision of education at all levels for all population groups should be identical with regard to curriculum. In a country such as South Africa with its heterogeneous cultural and social values it would be unfair to [exclude] cultural and social community values from the curriculum.

The *third guideline* [implies the need for] clarity concerning the *model* that will be used [to] determin[e] the quality of the benefits to be provided for a particular category of educational clients. . . . On the basis of available resources, the level of provision to date available to Whites only will have to be progressively adapted and reformed to a level that can be made available to all relevant groups of educational clients, regardless of race, colour, language, creed, area, or sex.

The most important implication of the *fourth guideline* is that educationally irrelevant inequalities that are evident in the provision of education should be identified as clearly as possible and eliminated through educational reforms. . . . The principle of justice requires that sound educational strategies be devised to compensate for genetic or environmental disadvantages in the system of education provision.

Recommendations on Priorities

A system for the provision of education that is aimed at the pursuit and achievement of equal standards in education cannot be accomplished immediately. However, this should not be used as an excuse for sluggish and feeble attempts. It is regarded as a bounden duty to commence with a practical programme as soon as possible and to move purposefully towards the ultimate objective. The series of recommendations contained in this report were made with a view to establishing a basis for such a programme. The recommendations relate to the whole system for the provision of education and it is regarded as desirable to indicate which recommendations should be implemented as soon as possible.

EDUCATION MANAGEMENT: INTERIM COUNCIL FOR EDUCATION

The restructuring of the system for the provision of education should occur with the highest degree of consultation and it is therefore recommended that

1. an Interim Council for Education be appointed by the Cabinet or by a Minister appointed by the Cabinet, within the next few months;

2. the Council be appointed for a maximum period of three years;

3. the function of the Council be to advise on the consideration and implementation of the recommendations of the HSRC investigation into education;

4. attention be paid particularly to the establishment of norms and standards for the provision of education in the RSA;

5. the Interim Council for Education be established through an act of Parliament;

6. the Cabinet appoint one Minister as its agent in the matter;

7. the proposed Council should have access to any data relevant to the execution of its function;

8. the Council report regularly to Parliament on its activities and the progress made.

EDUCATIONAL STRUCTURE

It is recommended that the following matters be given priority:

1. The progressive introduction of nine years' compulsory education, six years of which should be compulsory schooling devoted to basic education.

2. The introduction of a pre-basic bridging period aimed at school readiness as soon as possible where the need is the greatest.

3. The expansion of preparatory vocational education, in addition to preparatory academic education, to meet the manpower needs of the country.

4. The establishment as soon as possible of the necessary infrastructure for the provision of nonformal education.

5. The granting of the right to Councils of autonomous educational institutions in higher education to decide who should be admitted as students.

SUPPORTING SERVICES

Supporting services are of primary importance in the improvement of the provision of education and it is therefore recommended that the planning and establishment of a cooperative education service should be given priority.

Curriculum Services

The effectiveness of the pre-basic bridging period, basic education, differentiation at the senior intermediate level, the teaching of languages, the natural sciences, and mathematics, and the development of nonformal education is dependent on a thorough and expert curriculum design and development service. The service should not only be planned and provided on a national basis but should also be developed simultaneously at second level and local level by means of regional centres and within teacher centres. At national level the service should be provided on a contract basis.

The provision of the service at the national and second levels is dependent on the immediate training of curriculum specialists.

Educational-Technological Services

The role that educational technology can play in improving the quality of education, bridging the gaps, and expanding nonformal education has been indicated and it is felt that the service, together with the curriculum service at all three levels, should be developed. Action research on computer-assisted instruction and the involvement of the Post Office and the SABC should be given priority.

Guidance Services

The meaningfulness of decisions made by learners and their parents regarding learning or progress within a system of formal education, choice of fields of study in formal and nonformal education, etc., is dependent on well grounded guidance. Concentration on manpower needs and therefore actual job opportunities is a prerequisite for link[ing] education and work, which is why guidance, especially vocational guidance, is an essential service. It is therefore recommended that

1. a comprehensive guidance service should be developed at all three levels with the inclusion of the private sector;

2. recommendations on the training of school guidance officers and their career prospects should enjoy top priority.

Health and Social Services

The utilization of learning opportunities is also determined by the physical health and social well-being of the learner. It is therefore recommended that the necessary cooperation should be obtained, the infrastructure created progressively, and decisions made concerning the minimum standards so that this service for all learners can be placed on an acceptable level.

Evaluative and Diagnostic Services for Learners with Handicaps

The provision of services should be developed gradually as part of the total cooperative educational service as recommended, but the field training of professional staff and cooperation between medical, paramedical, psychological, social work, and pedagogical professional staff should be given priority.

A Cooperative Educational Service

The cooperative educational service should be developed simultaneously at the national or first level, the second level, and the third or local level. The actual operational levels, namely second and third levels, are dependent on sophisticated research and development assistance but should also be as close as possible to the user for effective rendering of services and involvement.

RECRUITMENT AND TRAINING OF TEACHERS

The key factor in the provision of education is the teacher. It is recommended that

1. a registration authority where all teaching staff may register should be instituted;

2. the registration authority should as its first priority after the necessary consultations decide on the categories in which teaching staff may register;

3. a model recruitment and selection programme should be developed for use by educational authorities after adaptations;

4. geographically well-situated institutions should be planned and constructed for groups requiring additional facilities, and that a training programme for the staff who are to man institutions of this kind should be implemented as soon as possible;

5. the training of teachers for general formative and preparatory career education (technical education in particular) should enjoy top priority;

6. the recommendations in respect of the training of teachers of the natural sciences and mathematics should receive immediate attention;

7. "Standard ten" as the minimum admission requirement for teacher training should be applied as soon as possible and that facilities for those wishing to obtain this qualification should be provided and the continuous need for in-service training satisfied;

8. statutory machinery for negotiation should be introduced;

9. the conditions of service should be improved to and maintained at a level that ensures reasonable numbers are drawn to the profession and the retention of serving teachers;

10. the coordination of training of teaching personnel should be one of the tasks of the proposed South African Council for Education.

PHYSICAL FACILITIES

The backlog with regard to the provision of the necessary facilities of an acceptable standard in respect of existing facilities, present shortages, and additional needs as a result of increased numbers is matter of extreme urgency. It is recommended that

1. national space and cost norms be established;

2. a survey should be made of underutilized and unused facilities after it has been decided if and to what extent the facilities can be used to solve problems created by shortages. The necessary steps should be taken to implement the decision in an effort to eliminate inequalities;

3. a study should be undertaken to ascertain where inadequate provision has been made and a plan drawn up to satisfy the needs by way of programmes according to acceptable norms and design criteria;

4. a structured national inventory of existing facilities should be compiled and kept up to date to assist in national planning;

5. a national budget programme should be drawn up in the light of the findings in respect of [recommendations] 1, 2, 3, and 4, the available means, and the recommendations on the financing of education that follow.

FINANCING OF EDUCATION

There is no doubt that the provision of education of equal quality will require more funds. Bearing in mind that means are not unlimited, it is recommended that

1. financially realistic norms for the provision of an adequate standard of education should be drawn up and revised from time to time by the central educational authority and should be used for the central authority's financing of education for the total population;

2. an effort should be made to aim at achieving parity in government expenditure on education over the shortest possible period on the basis of the norms proposed in [recommendation] 1, bearing in mind limitations in respect of budgets, manpower, etc.;

3. taking the aim in [recommendation] 2 as the point of departure, each educational authority should table its annual budget with a view to achieving parity within specified periods of time. The budget request should be coordinated centrally;

4. backlogs existing in comparison with the norm proposed in [recommendation] 1 should be estimated in respect of the

quantity and quality of school buildings, the qualifications of teaching staff, the ratio of pupils per teacher, and the salaries of teaching staff. Provision should also be made for eliminating backlogs within the shortest possible period with due consideration for budgetary and other restrictions;

5. a reliable statistical basis for the educational expenditure of the central government should be developed as soon as possible and used to promote and secure parity and enable a centralised evaluation of this progress to be made;

6. attention should be paid to the application of measures in education that will lead to better utilization of scarce resources (teachers, buildings, and grounds) in education;

7. the growth-dependent financing of universities should be reconsidered so that the pressure on recruitment of students can be reduced with a view to more rational canalization of learners towards preparatory career education instead of the present one-sided and excessive movement towards academic preparatory education.

PLANNING FOR THE PROVISION OF EDUCATION

A sophisticated and continuous survey of the need for and change in the demand for education as a result of, inter alia, trends in population growth and shifts and changing manpower needs should enjoy top priority as the basis for the flexible planning of the provision of education.

The Provisional Response of the Government to the de Lange Committee Report (1981)

The government released the (de Lange committee) report of the HSRC and its own initial response simultaneously. Commenting on the government's Interim Memorandum, *the text of which follows, HSRC committee member Franklin Sonn alleged: "This, in fact, reestablishes apartheid education and places us back where we started"* (Rand Daily Mail, *October 9, 1981).*

1. The Government wishes to express its appreciation of the extensive inquiry instituted by the Human Sciences Research Council into a system for the provision of education for all population groups in the Republic of South Africa. The inquiry covered a wide field, and the fact that the task was completed within the record time of thirteen months deserves special mention.

The Government wishes, too, to express its thanks to the literally hundreds of individuals who, it is clear from the Report, assisted in the inquiry, to the HSRC, which provided the expert guidance and made its scientific infrastructure available under the South African Plan for Research in the Human Sciences, and to Professor J. P. de Lange, who was Chairman of the Head Committee of the Inquiry.

The Government wishes to point out that the main report, entitled "The Provision of Education in the RSA," was subscribed to and signed by the HSRC and its Head Committee, but that the Head Committee does not necessarily associate itself with the recommendations in the eighteen supporting reports of the Working Committees.

As was stated in the terms of reference which the HSRC received from the Government in June 1980, the Government trusts that this inquiry will make a real contribution towards the improved provision of education in the RSA at all levels of education, in order to ensure that the potential of its inhabitants is realised, the economic growth of the RSA is promoted, its manpower needs are met, the quality of life of all its inhabitants is enhanced, and that education of equal quality is achieved for all population groups—all of this with due regard to the diversity of peoples in South African society and the resources available in the country's economy as a whole.

The Government sees the provision of education in the RSA as one of its top priorities and in this spirit will give urgent and serious attention to the findings and recommendations in the Report.

2. The Report contains numerous positive recommendations that will certainly promote the provision of education. That the Government is in earnest about the Report is evident from its statement that it accepts the [following] principles for the provision of education proposed in [chapter 2] of the Report, subject to points of departure already decided on by the Government which are set out in paragraph 3 below. The Government would emphasise that these principles are to be understood in context with one another and that no one principle is to be interpreted on its own in isolation. The principles concerned are the following:

□ *Principle 1*. Equal opportunities for education, including equal standards in education, for every inhabitant, irrespective of race, colour, creed, or sex, shall be the purposeful endeavour of the State.

□ *Principle 2*. Education shall afford positive recognition of what is common as well as what is diverse in the religious and cultural way of life and the languages of the inhabitants.

□ *Principle 3*. Education shall give positive recognition to the freedom of choice of the individual, parents, and organisations in society.

□ *Principle 4*. The provision of education shall be directed in an educationally responsible manner to meet the needs of the individual as well as those of society and economic development, and shall, inter alia, take into consideration the manpower needs of the country.

□ *Principle 5*. Education shall endeavour to achieve a positive relationship between the formal, nonformal, and informal aspects of education in the school, society, and family.

□ *Principle 6*. The provision of formal education shall be a responsibility of the State provided that the individual, parents, and organized society shall have a shared responsibility, choice, and voice in this matter.

□ *Principle 7*. The private sector and the state shall have a shared responsibility for the provision of nonformal education.

□ *Principle 8*. Provision shall be made for the establishment and state subsidisation of private education within the system of providing education.

□ *Principle 9*. In the provision of education the processes of centralization and decentralization shall be reconciled organizationally and functionally.

□ *Principle 10*. The professional status of the teacher and lecturer shall be recognized.

□ *Principle 11*. Effective provision of education shall be based on continuing research.

3. There are, however, certain aspects and possible implications of the Report about which the Government has reservations. Accordingly the Government has decided to lay down the following guiding principles as points of departure in the consideration of the Report.

□ The Report distinguishes between the principles for the provision of education in the RSA, which it proposes, and the more philosophical connotation of "principles of education," which it does not go into. In the light of this, the Government reaffirms that it stands by the principles of the Christian character and the broad national character of education as formulated in section 2 (1) (a) and (b) of the National Education Policy Act, 1967 (Act 39 of 1967), in regard to White education and as applied in practice or laid down in legislation in regard to the other population groups. Any changes or renewal in the provision of education will have to take these principles into account, with due regard to the right of self-determination which is recognised by Government policy for each population group.

□ The Government remains convinced that the principle of mother-tongue education is pedagogically valid, but appreciates that in the case of certain population groups the question of the language medium in teaching may give rise to particular problems of a special nature.

□ The Government reaffirms that, in terms of its policy that each population group should have its own schools, it is essential that each population group should also have its own education authority/department. The need for coordination is recognised, but this policy will have to be duly taken into account in any proposals relating to structures for central coordination and cooperation between the educational structures for the various population groups, and also in any proposals relating to educational structures at the regional or local levels. Education departments of their own are also essential to do justice to the right of self-determination which is recognised by Government policy for each population group.

□ The Government finds acceptable the principle of freedom of choice for the individual and for parents in educational matters and in the choice of a career, but within the framework of the policy that each population group is to have its own schools.

□ All decisions taken in terms of the recommendations in the Report will have to take due account of, and fit in with, the constitutional framework within which they are to be implemented.

4. In considering the findings and recommendations in the Report, the Government will concentrate mainly on the further improvement of the quality of education in the RSA and achieving education of equal quality for all population groups. The Government will not take any decisions on the recommendations in the Report until interested parties have had the opportunity of commenting and the Government has had a chance to consider thoroughly both the recommendations and the comments. On the basis of the guiding principles it has already decided on, as set out in paragraph 3, the Government will in due course take its stand on all the recommendations in the Report in a White Paper to be tabled in Parliament.

All official and recognised education bodies may submit their comments through the prescribed channels before 31 March 1982, and all other persons and organisations may send their comments direct to the Director-General: National Education, Private Bag X122, Pretoria, 0001.

5. For the coordinated consideration and possible implementation of the recommendations in the Report by the Government, the Minister of National Education will act as the convener of the three responsible Ministers, namely the Ministers of Internal Affairs, of Education and Training, and of National Education. These Ministers will be advised by an interim Education Working Party consisting of the heads of all education departments (both central and provincial), the Chairmen of the

National Education Council, the Council for Education and Training, and the Education Council (Coloureds), a nominated educationist in respect of the Indians, for whom there is no Education Council, the Chairman of the Committee of University Principals, the Chairman of the Committee of University Rectors, and the Rector of the University of the Western Cape. The Department of National Education will provide the Secretariat for the Education Working Party.

DOCUMENT VII:

Black Educators and White Institutions:

An Address by Professor Es'kia Mphahlele (1980)

In setting forth the case for American-style community colleges, Es'kia Mphahlele argues that even if English-medium, white universities were to be racially open, they could not meet the needs of African higher education. He set forth his views in the following (slightly abridged) graduation address published by the University of Witwatersrand Gazette *in July 1980.*

Black persons teaching or studying in a white university like Wits must constantly ask themselves what they are contributing to that makes any cultural sense. The answers are loaded with irony, rationalisings, with compromise. Once an institution has hired a person, presumably on the strength of his or her qualifications rather than as a case for sheltered employment, it is humiliating for such a person to be given a rank with a designation that sounds like *fanakalo*. For instance, why are some people called tutors and others lecturers?

Even when all the rating procedures have been judiciously dealt with, the nagging questions remain for a black student, and the black teacher at Wits: what does a Wits education say about my culture in a fragmented society? What can I contribute, if anything, to a society torn asunder by political authority, a society writhing in agony the immensity of which it is only dimly aware of? What can I do in an institution which the majority of my people are forbidden to enter that can benefit them? The black person who is in administration or is classified as "labourer" will meet the same problems that confront others who work in a white institution anywhere. But those who teach, be it in African languages, black literature, social work, or any other discipline, cannot even pretend that they are on a civilising mission among whites. These teachers are less than peripheral to the students' prospective careers. Even if the students feel increased by our teaching, it is a most uncertain investment, because we represent no political or economic force; also because Wits has put off for too long any serious programme of Africanisation in the content and thrust of its disciplines.

For a black person to pretend that teaching white people is a way of promoting the noblest tradition of "universal education" as distinct from "black" or "white" education is to fly in the face of history at a time when the majority of blacks and whites, including those who run our lives, are far from ready for it.

Ready? The word is crucial on this very campus. I am fully aware that the vice-chancellor and part of his administration are ready for dramatic changes. They try to keep their ear to the ground in order to listen to the needs of black education. And I happen to know that the vice-chancellor is concerned that Wits should snap out of its narcissistic cocoon to reach out to the larger South African community. Already we have an office for special projects which concerns itself with bridging courses for students who need assistance in adjusting to a university career, with teaching programmes outside the university framework, e.g., the upgrading of English teachers in Soweto and so on.

The Centre for Continuing Education is conducting courses it is hoped will now attract more black students than has hitherto been the case. These must now move into the urban townships for easier accessibility. There are other outreach postures that are still tentative and clumsy, provoked by irresistible institutions outside of Wits, and which one suspects the university is adopting just so as to be seen to be "involved." The vice-chancellor's efforts need more radical and widespread support. Wits can do infinitely better with mid-career courses, e.g., trade union organising, community health, nutrition, community organisation, and so on, for the enrichment of the working person's knowledge and skills. The venue must be in the townships, the courses must be community-centred. But one senses somewhere inside this institution an almost irreducible core of conservatism or orthodoxy, even racism, that smells like the old-fashioned liberalism of the Phillipses, the Hoernles, and the mission churches, even while it would like to appear scholarly and "enlightened." A conservatism that wants to "accommodate," "contain" within the framework of political sanctions the clamour of the black millions pounding on the gates with their fists and clubs, shaking them and yelling to be let in. They say they have no education? Let them get a degree! I can hear a voice say from an inner chamber. This resistance comes from the lower strata of the administration—some deans and some heads of departments. It is the old game of accommodating a black presence without the desire to change the existing structures demanded by such a presence, or to go beyond certain limits in the special programmes that are provided.

Some departments easily fall into the pattern of most English-medium universities in this country, who structure their syllabuses as if South Africa were not on the African continent. This cheats even the white students out of a rich and relevant heritage.

Related to these shortcomings is the fact that even were Wits, Cape Town, Rhodes, Natal, to open their doors to more qualified blacks tomorrow, this would still fall short of the number of students who want to pursue a post-secondary career. Black students would still be minority groups in the white universities. Would staff and students be ready for the residential and social mixing that are the corollary of the interracial learning environment?

The American experiment in interracial learning offers some hard lessons for us. The most important one is that there are black students who go to a white university all keyed up to survive the inevitable psychological experience of a minority status. They do this in order to assert their constitutional right to attend any institution of their choice. The minority status involves a degree of surrender to the cultural and political supremacy of the majority group. For this reason, black students invariably regroup to form a caucus to protect that distinctive world view and self-image that go with the historical condition of blackness. These tensions arise basically because North American whites are on the one hand a racist society and on the other an open one in which the constitutional machinery affords the black man a fighting chance to assert his civil rights. The student who does not want to be involved in minority politics on campus and/or cannot afford the cost of schooling in a white university goes to a predominantly black school or one with a huge black population, such as a state university.

Wits wants jealously to guard its standards and its ethnocentric curricula and will take in black students strictly on its own terms. While we would like to increase considerably its intake of black students, it would be arrogant for Wits to imagine that all of us want a university education at *any* cost, at *any* white university, including being sucked into an institution that has generally been slow to Africanise its character.

In view of all this I should like to see a college in or near Soweto that can unreservedly meet our needs as blacks, address our distinctive educational problems, ease the slower student into the mainstream without making him or her feel like a subject of therapy.

I favour the American style of community college. It is non-residential and functions day and night. It provides terminal and preparatory two-year programmes for the student who may not necessarily want a degree and the one who does and may thus transfer to a full-fledged university to finish. It provides mid-career programmes in technology, commerce, nursing, teacher training, home economics, and others, tailored for immediate community services. Such a college will be acceptable to Africans only if it has a black principal and a black council with no more government representation than white universities have. Faculty and student exchange between such a community college and Wits would help shape it into a viable institution. Right from the ground floor of its construction, the community college should consciously stay clear of the kind of political ideology that bedevils the operation of all the black universities to a point of stagnation, where they are now a travesty of higher learning.

This college can become a centre for Soweto's cultural life and fulfilment in every sense of the term "culture." The nearest example of a university that serves this function for another community is the Rand Afrikaans University—an institution which expresses the cultural aspirations of the Afrikaner and may yet become the instrument of refinement among Afrikaners beyond its immediate environment. Africans have no such university that expresses their own personality.

The Future of the Urban University in South Africa:

Some Practical Considerations by F. M. Orkin, L. O. Nicolaysen, and Max Price (1978)

In 1978 two faculty members, F. M. Orkin and L. O. Nicolaysen, and a student, Max Price, at the University of Witwatersrand co-authored a provocative article on what the future urban university in South Africa ought to be like. The article was subsequently published in the University of Cape Town's social science journal, Social Dynamics *(vol. 5, no. 1, June 1979). The abridged text follows. Note that the authors use the term "Black" to denote black African.*

In a spirited riposte, "Open Minds and Closed Systems: Comments on the Functions and Future of the 'Urban' 'English-Speaking' University in South Africa," published in Social Dynamics *(vol. 6, no. 2, December 1980), J. H. Keenan, also of the University of Witwatersrand, asserts that such universities are instruments of capitalist control and class domination.*

Introduction

What are the factors which a university like our own should take into account when considering its future in a South African setting, and what should its response to them be? Our remarks are most obviously applicable to urban universities situated in industrial complexes, notably the Universities of the Witwatersrand, Natal (Durban), Cape Town, and Port Elizabeth; and we expect that our framework of debate will be most familiar to English-speaking colleagues. But many of our proposals would have implications for the university community as a whole, and the topic itself is of general interest, since this kind of exercise— already well under way in Zimbabwe, and being undertaken in Namibia—will obviously become of increasing importance in South Africa.

First we note some changes in this society [that] are almost inexorable. Second we argue that if universities want to play a constructive part in the changes while promoting those of their present features that are desirable, they will have to alter their character significantly. Third we look elsewhere for existing university models which could guide us, and find little that is helpful. So, in the fourth section, we propose instead a basic outlook: the university must seek to participate in the future of South Africa rather than be dragged through it. This outlook allows us to formulate some aims for, and consider some constraints on, the university. Against this background we develop in the last section some broad features for the future structure of curricula, professional degrees, and the research orientation and interaction with its community, of the urban university.

Features of Any South African Future

South Africa's future may take several forms, but all of them must begin from certain brute facts:

1. The races in SA are now divided by staggering economic and educational inequality: average White per capita income was R182 per month in 1975 and Black, R12.50—a ratio of 14:1. There is a further, widening division between urban and rural Blacks—the income ratio has increased by 18 percent over the

last decade, up to 2.8:1. The White population is much more urbanized, entrepreneurial, and economically related to the rest of the world than the Black population.

2. A vast population explosion is already irreversibly under way. The present rate of increase of the Black population is twice that of the White, even though the Black infant mortality rate is five times higher (94 vs. 19 infants per 1000 from 1970–75). So by 2000 there will be 7m Whites (provided net immigration keeps up), 37m Blacks and 5m others. Blacks will then outnumber Whites in ostensibly "White" [urban areas] by 3:1, yet the majority of Blacks will still be on the land.

3. Urbanization, involving a change in living standards and a greater likelihood of education, significantly reduces the Black urban birth rate. But there is no comparable effect for the rural group, where any increase in overall income is offset by the extra mouths to feed, so that increase in per capita income (which is important for population growth rate to slow) is not achieved. Thus a vicious circle of mutually reinforcing poverty and fertility exists in the rural areas, set in motion and sustained by the use of these areas as dormitories for the industrial centres and dumping grounds for the unemployed.

4. The proportion of young in the overall Black population is higher than in the White (44 percent vs. 31 percent under 14 years).

5. Total Black unemployment is estimated to have risen to between 15 and 20 percent. The highest percentages are found among those in the 16–24-year-old category, and among those with no education or only primary education. Evidently, then, the tendency will continue that the highest unemployment rate is borne by young black school leavers.

6. The government's Economic Development Programme for 1976–78 stressed that a minimal annual growth rate of 5 percent was necessary to meet the employment demands of the rapidly growing (2.7 percent p.a.) labour force and make any headway with the backlog. These are long-term figures, whereas the growth rate of the economy can fluctuate. But as a

recent indication, real GDP only grew by 1.5 percent in 1976, and estimates were that it would not grow by more than 3–4 percent over the programming period.

7. Apart from our own peculiarities, we share with other less developed countries the problem of industrializing in economic competition with the fully developed, mass-producing Western nations and Japan. So SA will continue to face harsh competition in international trade.

8. The foregoing will, on any version of SA's future, encourage accelerated exploitation of our natural resources, in order to earn foreign reserves and to create local employment, by which to increase the Black standard of living and so also reduce the population growth rate. So we must expect far greater hazards to our environment during this period of accelerated resource development whose consequences would be as grave as hunger and social dislocation are now.

9. SA is now in the spotlight of world opinion, and more importantly of superpower politics. This does not affect what we ought to do, but will magnify the consequences of whatever we decide to do.

How Will This Future Develop?

There are a number of conceivable scenarios for the course of South Africa's future development, which one may group under two broad headings:

1. It will industrialize on the Western pattern.
2. It will develop on an African pattern, either capitalist industrialization as in Nigeria or Rhodesia or socialist development (not necessarily emphasizing industrialization) as in Tanzania or Mozambique.

Urban universities, especially those English-language universities situated in the major industrialized centres of Johannesburg, Durban, and Cape Town, will be tempted to assume scenario 1 in their planning for the future. But our central contention is that the kinds of future that are still feasible, very different though they may be, fall under scenario 2 rather than 1.

Scenario 1 may nevertheless be of partial use in thinking about the development of the highly industralized regions which immediately surround these urban universities. For example, two-thirds of the economically active people at present in metropolitan Johannesburg are Black, Coloured, or Indian. Given that influx control is unlikely to be fully maintained, the White proportion will probably decline to something like one-fourth of the economically active persons. So the respective industrial communities will largely be composed of people to many of whom industry, economic development, and education will be relatively new. There will still be great cultural and linguistic diversity, whatever political developments may come about. The universities must be willing to recognize this diversity in their composition and operation.

Now these industrialized regions are themselves surrounded by the country at large. In [the year] 2000 the countryside will still contain 22m of our fellow South Africans. This is where we must draw on scenario 2, and the emphases placed, for example, by Nigeria or Tanzania on rural development. For it would be irresponsible to pretend that the urban areas are self-sufficient. For example, up to 40 percent of the urban Black workforce is migrant labour from the rural areas. So the universities must recognize the problems [of] the *relation* of the industrialized regions to the rural surroundings and their considerable responsibility in the latter's development.

These scenarios have identified what kind of future South Africa might face. We do not yet know *how* one or the other might come about. Scenario 1 relies on the "logic of industrialism." On this view, racially discriminatory measures, which are inefficient as well as unjust, will be inexorably swept aside by growing demands of the market for a skilled and mobile workforce.

There are two standard competing views for the mechanism of scenario 2. On the one view, industrialisation in racial contexts accommodates itself to, rather than breaks down, existing racial practices: unless, of course, key figures in the process—businessmen and professionals—can be prevailed upon to act liberally, and reap the benefits of ultimately greater efficiency. On this view, the university's contribution to the future would require that it explicitly encourage in its students a commitment to achieving a nonracial society. . . .

On the second view, [post-colonial] industrialization [need not be fashioned] by the innovations of enlightened employers. [It may be formed by] the demands of their exploited employees. In this case, the university's contribution to development would involve a reorientation towards the interests of the latter.

It is not easy to establish at this stage—indeed, there is disagreement between the authors—which of the two mechanisms will bring scenario 2 about. But the point is this: whichever mechanism operates, if a university wishes to help rather than hinder the process it will have to make a far-reaching commitment to achieving a more equitable and nonracial society.

This conclusion is further supported by some insights of development economics. We noted [above] the relation between the developed and the underdeveloped areas of SA. This implies that if the production of material necessities in the latter is to overtake the increase of population, production will have to be fundamentally reorganized as well as accelerated. What the universities can contribute is training and research specifically oriented towards the underdeveloped areas. . . .

On either account students will have to be confronted with these facts about inequalities and imbalances in the context of their future lives. They will then perceive that their university's commitment to the achievement of a nonracial South Africa is not just political theory but vital for a viable future.

Should We Seek Out Other Universities as Models?

Where, then, might we look for a comprehensive model for the role which the urban university will play, not only in the development of its industrialized environment but in the relation of the latter to the development of the country? The answer we suggest is: nowhere, really. We can draw on other models in selected respects; but we contend the South African situation will require a unique configuration, which we are largely going to have to sort out for ourselves.

1. Why should we not look to Western universities? The trend this century has been towards the narrowing in Europe of class inequalities in access to education. But the pace has been slow. Thus, of UK working class children born in the 1930s only 1 1/2 percent obtained a university education; for working class children born in 1953–54, the proportion has increased to 4 percent (compared to 18 percent for children of middle class families and 35 percent for children of upper-middle class, professional families). If the university is to contribute to a moderately just society, especially in respect of educational opportunity, there is not time to act at that pace.

2. Why it is not especially helpful to look to African universities

  (a) We should look to the University of Dar es Salaam in Tanzania for the commitment a developing country may demand of its students: partly by the large component of *any* degree devoted to the compulsory study of relevant aspects of the prevailing social reality; and partly by requiring students to repay their time at university by working for a period in the public service, preferably in a rural area. Where the analogy tends to fail for us is that Tanzania is a one-party, one-university country in which there is high congruence between national and university goals. The same would apply to Mozambique.

  (b) The University at Lagos in Nigeria provides a much closer analogy [to existing urban universities in SA], so much so that it is not particularly suggestive. Lagos University was founded as an explicitly urban enterprise; and it even has much the same facilities as the urban universities here.

  (c) The University of Rhodesia [openly opposes] a race-oriented regime; [but] while a majority of the undergraduates were Black by 1976, only 6 percent of the academic staff and 4 percent of the administrative were Black (though these percentages have been increasing fast lately). Initially far too few of its Black students entered technology and the professions.

3. Other universities: Countries like Taiwan, Singapore, and Costa Rica have at least achieved *economic* growth. Selected aspects of education and technical training in these countries might provide useful insights. But the *nature* of economic development there and its relation to social goals need critical consideration.

Constraints and Aims of University Development in South Africa

We have gained no more than some pointers from what universities in other situations do. We shall thus fall back on what we think we *ought* to do, within a framework we must now try to define.

EXTERNAL CONSTRAINTS

1. How many university students is South Africa likely to need, and can it afford to produce them? Consider the third or fourth columns of Table 1, which gives the data for 1974. It makes clear that the [percentage] of South Africa's White population at university is higher than in every developed country shown, bar the US; while the [percentage] of her Black population at university is similar to that in underdeveloped Ghana. The overall [percentage] for South Africa is similar to that in the UK and half that of an industrializing country like Spain.

SA needs more intermediate professional and technical degrees; so she probably ought not allow the present overall [percentage]. [But] we will probably not be able to afford a much greater [percentage] than Spain's. So, since the population will have doubled by [the year] 2000, we can expect to need between two and four times the present *number* of university places by then.

What of the racial distribution of places? Let us suppose that the country's immediate priority should be development to

TABLE 1

1974	Students at university and equivalent[1] institutions	National population (thousands)	Students per ten thousand population	Students per thousand of 20–24 year olds[2]
Tanzania	2,644	14,763	1.8	2.0
Nigeria	23,228	61,270	3.8	4.8
SA (Africans)	7,845	17,745	4.4	5.7
Ghana	5,625	9,607	5.9	–
Singapore[3]	8,142	2,219	37	34
SA (Overall)	110,808	24,920	45	61
Britain[3]	228,057	55,968	51	70
Spain	304,532	35,225	87	129
W. Germany	641,243	62,041	103	158
Australia[3]	142,859	13,339	107	125
Costa Rica	28,230	1,921	147	154
Japan	1,762,040	109,671	161	181
SA (whites)	95,589	4,160	230	280
United States	6,912,182	211,909	326	362[4]

SOURCE: Compiled from the *Unesco Statistical Yearbook, 1976,* and from the SAIRR *Survey of Race Relations in South Africa, 1974.*

1. E.g. polytechnics in Germany and France but not in Britain (cf. note 3 below).

2. This column shows that the proportion of students at university and equivalent institutions in their age cohort quite closely follows the proportion in the overall population.

3. The above table is for students at university and equivalent institutions, not for students in tertiary education in general. The two figures differ by less than 25% of the latter in all the countries listed, except for Britain, Singapore and Australia. In these three cases the figure for tertiary education in general is approximately double the figure for university and equivalent institutions as specified above. So if one uses these three countries to estimate a desirable university ratio for SA, one should weight the specified ratio upwards.

4. The figure for students in tertiary education in general in the USA is 536 per thousand of 20–24 year olds, i.e. a majority of the age cohort. This figure has stabilised, and is thought to be the maximum attainable.

provide productive employment for predominantly unskilled Blacks. The process will demand a range of skills among job-creators and employees—e.g., to innovate and execute labour-intensive patterns in industry and agriculture while maintaining a competitive position in international trade—together with the professional and technical services such social and economic development will demand. . . . We can expect that by [the year] 2000 much of universities' *increase* in size will represent Black intake and that (as in Rhodesia) Blacks will ultimately outnumber Whites. There will be intense and fully justified pressure from Black youth, their parents, and their political leaders for more urban university places. What [can] we start doing *now* to meet this need? We must not only respond, but be seen to respond.

2. Where might our Black students come from? One might expect in the long term that the composition of the university student populations might roughly reflect that of the overall population. [For this to happen,] both the quantity and quality of Black secondary education will have to improve dramatically. What might this involve? [It would involve quadrupling the number of Black secondary students, more than doubling expenditures on education, and training a quarter of a million Black teachers.]

The implication seems unavoidable. Even on a fundamental reconsideration of national priorities, South Africa could hardly afford to extend schooling on the present White pattern to Black pupils in an equitable way. Since systematic discrimination is unacceptable, the present White pattern of schooling will have to be fundamentally changed.

The universities could make a twofold contribution to the problem. Firstly, they could provide crash programmes for producing and upgrading Black teachers, to help increase the output of Black matriculants. Secondly, they could provide for Black adults wanting to do part-time degrees in preference to doing a correspondence course through UNISA. These would be mature, motivated, valuable students. The universities should make more courses, especially for teachers and the new intermediate courses we propose below, [available] part-time. This would allow a large increase in enrollments without a correspondingly large outlay on new premises and buildings.

3. Effective progress towards the achievement of a nonracial society demands some sort of affirmative action at least in the short term. Admission policy [should be] coupled with special courses to make up for deficiencies most notable in, but not confined to, the Black school system. Such courses would accordingly be required of *all* students below a certain qualifying standard.

4. The question of affirmative action also applies, even more controversially, to staff appointments. The standard arguments against it weigh more heavily here. But given the emphasis on locally oriented curricula which we urge below, one might expect that in many cases not only the best but the only academically qualified staff would be black. On the administrative side, to give an example, more senior secretarial or administrative posts [may be advertised] in predominantly White-readership newspapers. Such practices should be revised.

5. The above three points have dealt with criteria used here or overseas for selecting members of a university. New criteria also need to be considered—e.g., selecting students, academic staff, etc. according to their readiness to undertake, as part of their coursework [and] duties, an involvement with their community. This move would guarantee that they did not enter the university with a view to using their qualifications simply as a passport to move overseas. . . .

6. The universities will need Black leaders [to] perceive the importance of high academic and communitarian standards in the university and argue for them to be maintained. We need to bring Black community and political leaders into high-level advisory roles in our university without delay—e.g., on the governing councils [and] selection committees for chairs.

INTERNAL CONSTRAINTS

It may be plausibly argued that many departments in our universities are presently of less than "critical size," e.g., they cannot offer enough options; they struggle when a member of staff goes on leave; there is not enough diversity of interest for staff research seminars. Given lots more students in general, these departments would be allocated their proportion of new posts, and eventually reach critical size. This is then an argument for university growth across the board.

But our theme has been that South Africa cannot afford more than twice the present [percentage] of students [in] the overall population. As we saw, since the population will double by [the year] 2000, the overall university population should be two to four times the present size by [then]. But what of departments that are then still sub-critical? Clearly, the provision of departments and even faculties will have to be coordinated among universities in some workable configuration, thereby avoiding the needless duplication of sub-critical departments that exists at the moment.

AIMS

It would demand a separate paper to consider the guiding moral aims of a university which sought to help in achieving and maintaining a good society. We shall confine ourselves to listing the few very general principles which our argument so far has implicitly invoked:

(a) At the individual level, education involves the acquiring of some specified corpus of knowledge, and the learning of associated cognitive or practical skills. The point of education at this level is primarily that the individual in realising his characteristic aptitudes, usually in interaction with others, enhances both his and their human well-being in a shared social context; the point is not that he can thereby earn more.

(b) At the social level, therefore, the university would want there to be equitable access to its opportunities for educational self-realization. This aim requires firstly that the competition for university places be fair; so that the university would try—in its own programmes, and through what influence it can exert on the school and social system—to eliminate, and otherwise to compensate for, disadvantages in the home background of its present and prospective students. Secondly, the university would have to offer scholarships for students who might not apply because they could not afford to take up the places they would win.

(c) At a political level, the university would want to realise its own institutional destiny in social interaction; not only by reaping the benefits when its chosen goals happen to coincide with social imperatives, but by participating in the genuinely national debate about what [its goals] should be and how they can best be achieved.

Broad Features of the Future of the Urban University, as Governed by Aims and Constraints

The guidelines for the future have been set, then, by the demands of a modicum of social justice; what just distribution of educational resources South Africa can afford; and the kind of future development of the country within which these have to be achieved. Working within these guidelines we must take account of the situation of the urban universities in the middle of the industrial powerhouses of the country, which are in turn significantly fuelled by the rural majority of the country. The universities, especially the English-language ones, have hitherto shaped themselves along *laissez-faire* Western lines; but now must help meet the daunting challenges of the South African future.

The functions of the university as traditionally conceived are the seeking and transmitting of knowledge. But these two functions have always been modified by a third, the production of skilled manpower: originally for the church, then for industry and the private professions, and most recently also for the range of technical and specialised occupations required in the civil services of a modern state. So what is crucial is the balance which each university, in its particular context, will choose to strike between two extremes: on the one hand, research and teaching for their own sake; and on the other hand, research directed towards resolving the debates and solving the problems of national development, and the training of technical and professional manpower.

The balance we propose involves the following:

1. *The university as a forum.* The South Africa we have sketched is a troubled society overdue for change, yet chronically divided as to how to achieve it. There are too few institutions fostering regular analysis and informed debate on the divisive issues. Even for the moment, when the institutional role of the English-language university in particular is mainly oppositional, it should participate constructively, with its constituency, by inviting community leaders and public figures to articulate their policies and proposals. In doing so we should aim to coax all of our staff and the student body into rationally assessing even unpopular opinions. Subsequently we might hope that the commitment to achieving a nonracial society which we espouse as an institution will, partly through our own efforts, be more widely shared. The university would then expect to play an influential consultative role in initiating, as well as analysing and responding to, public policy.

2. *The role of research.* Our ability to conduct vigorous independent inquiry becomes increasingly important with people having to introduce and adjust to fundamental social changes, while all the time our society becomes more crowded and our environment and resources come under pressure. Thus two complex questions of priorities need fresh and concerted debate: research versus other social needs; and pure research versus applied research. Their complexity is highlighted by the following, which need to be incorporated into the standard debates.

On the first question, one should note that a developing country may attach as much significance as a developed one to the creative achievements of its own scholars, scientists, and artists. The community feels validated in its standing in the world, and the consequent gain in self-respect is an important part of the development process. Work of true distinction will have this value even if it does not have practical import. However, even the prestige-value of distinguished research will not justify our spending vast sums on esoteric "big science" of the kind that even the developed Western societies can no longer afford.

On the second question, one should note that research that is applied is not ipso facto applicable to local needs. Some aspects of high technology do appear to be important for the future: say, the mastery of fuel synthesis. On the other hand, there is a strong tendency to build up high-technology enclaves which widen the gap between the enclave-dwellers, ourselves, and those affected by the symptoms of structured underdevelopment—poverty and overpopulation. We should rather weight our efforts towards [projects that] narrow the gap: for example, research on [practical] birth control methods, the physiology of malnutrition, solar energy utilization, and land deterioration in the tribal areas; and, at a [more] general level, research on the processes which relate the development of the urban areas to the underdevelopment of the rural areas and legitimize the relationship in terms of racial ideology.

In general we must discover how the country ticks while deciding how best we can guide its development towards what we believe is desirable. Our own university, for example, surely needs an adequately funded, problem-oriented, interdisciplinary centre for contemporary social research. Such a centre would allow it to fulfil the commitment towards achieving a viable nonracial future—by undertaking comprehensive and above all locally-committed projects, by recognizing both the urban nature of its immediate environment and its ties to the rural areas, and by fostering debate, broad-based consultation, and community involvement in urban and national planning. We would hope that other universities would in a similar way identify areas of need which they are suited, but are failing, to meet. . . .

3. *Professional and technical training.* The University of Ibadan had a classics department for ten years before it taught agriculture or law. Our own University has from the outset been mostly a technical and professional training institution (this would apply to other urban universities to varying extents, given their particular history and present situation). So it is easier for us, at least, than for African universities that adopted the idea of a

British arts-and-science university, to give due attention to the professional needs of the community. But who is the community? Taking our University as a probably representative example, the constitution of its governing council suggests, and the content and structure of curricula in law, engineering, medicine, business, and so on confirm, that the community which the university sees itself as serving is in the main White and wealthy.

4. *Teaching*. To meet the commitment we have argued for, we need to teach labour law as well as corporation law; preventive medicine for Black communities as well as the intensive care of White individuals; rural development economics as well as marketing management; the design of low-cost housing as well as highrise office blocks; and so on.

But [the problems on] which the university will be working can only be effectively tackled in a coordinated fashion. [Their] resolution will demand the effective integration of an appropriate interdisciplinary component in each course (rather than a few lectures not for credit, tacked on as an afterthought). This will mean a lot of new work for lecturing staff, a lot more team-teaching, and a freer flow of students between departments, plus an administration interested, flexible, and responsive enough to handle the ensuing complexity.

These curricula will get off the ground at all, and then avoid degenerating into academic chat, only if one can guarantee a system of fruitful involvement with the real needs of communities. . . . What the country really needs, we contend, are more medically skilled, technically skilled, administratively skilled people at an intermediate rather than a fully professional level. . . .

Tak[ing] medicine as an example, how would one arrange to teach intermediate professionals in suitable numbers, while guaranteeing the connection with the community that is their raison d'être? One way would be to make the intermediate qualifications leading to a final medical degree cumulative, and separated by mandatory stints in the community which count as a qualifying part of each degree. Thus, the graduate doctor will have done, say, the same initial eighteen months, plus a six-month stint in the community, as a health official who does not proceed further. And he will have done the same next two years, plus a further one-year stint in the community, as a medical officer who does not proceed further. The more purely medical component of each year would increase as the student moves further through the overall programme. One would expect students of various experience and all ages at each stage of the course; and one need not limit first-year admissions to students wealthy enough to envisage several successive years out of work.

The final product will be equal in the rigour of his thought and skill to the doctor trained overseas; and vastly superior in the variety and depth of his practical experience; but the content of his training will not be comparable, since it will have been so closely linked to local requirements and research. This will, of course, solve at a stroke the problem of South African doctors training here in order to leave immediately for overseas. They simply won't be able to, and anyone explicitly planning to go overseas would as little do medicine or engineering with that in mind as they would now do law.

It might be argued against this scheme that the training for the respective jobs will have to be qualitatively as well as quantitatively different, so that if the training of the final doctor is not to suffer, the universities must retain discrete courses for each category (perhaps lodging the most junior courses in neighbouring colleges for advanced technology). This alternative is equally plausible. Moreover, it might not require a substantial increase in the overall medical slice of the economic pie. For the extra teachers and facilities needed to train adequate numbers of health assistants and medical officers (and similar dental officers) in discrete courses could be made available by combining the reduced numbers of actual medical and dental students in large classes in junior years.

We envisage comparable restructuring, on one or other arrangement, of the other professional degrees: e.g., supplementing fewer engineers with greater numbers of technologists and technicians; fewer lawyers with greater numbers of legal officials to handle routine procedures; fewer architects with greater numbers of housing advisers trained to meet the particular requirements of townships and villages, etc. In each case work in the community would count for credit toward completing each stage; and—especially with the help of evening classes—one would expect adults, armed with invaluable experience, seeking to further their studies throughout their working lives.

Conclusion

Some of our suggestions are controversial; better ones can probably be developed. Moreover, our argument may be less than uniformly coherent, because it represents compromises of perspective and opinion. But within the situation we have identified, any workable planning will [draw on] suggestions [like ours]. In each case what must be considered is not only a most desirable solution in our likely future context, but what we must start doing right now towards getting there.

What we are basically advocating is this: the university must change its ethos. We must become primarily orientated towards South Africa, and only then towards the international university and professional communities. The university is an engine of development, whether we like it or not. So let us direct it with rational planning and determined action. In doing so, we must accept the responsibilities we have in regard to the gross tasks of South Africa's future. Otherwise, we shall be taking a seat on the sidelines of the country's future, from which to shout inappropriate or even harmful advice. If that is all the participation we are prepared to aim at, we do not need to plan at all.

The Inaugural Address of Dr. Stuart J. Saunders, Principal of the University of Cape Town (1981)

Universalist in vision, Dr. Saunders' inauguration address of March 20, 1981, dealt with social values and intellectual themes in a manner both familiar and congenial to American academics. Acknowledging the importance of internal issues such as the need to foster excellence in teaching as well as research, he stressed the importance of the university's social responsibilities. The abridged text follows.

No Holy Cows

It is proper that universities should try to help solve the important issues facing the community, or communities, around them. In doing so they must seek the truth and enunciate it clearly. There can be no "Holy Cows" immune to their analysis and criticism. Some would stress the necessity of looking at local issues to the extent that only what is termed "relevant research" is undertaken. Such people tend to be disdainful of more fundamental research, which they regard as being esoteric. Some caution is necessary here. . . . To insist on relevant research implies that relevance is known and identifiable. It implies that inquiring minds can be directed. I reject such notions, but fully acknowledge that resources must be made available to help resolve immediate pressing problems, as long as the approaches to the solutions are not prescribed. The University has to help to solve our dependence on imported oil, and it is doing so. It has to enlarge the knowledge of our seas and shores and identify their commercial potential, and it is doing so. It has to eliminate and ameliorate diseases common in South Africa, and it is doing so. Our engineers and scientists are grappling with industrial problems, the Commerce Faculty is manifestly contributing to the business community. Research in the Law Faculty has contributed significantly to new laws, our educationists have been working to influence and update the curriculum, in the performing arts new insights have enriched cultural life, and the Faculties of Arts, Social Science, Architecture, and Science have scholars seeking answers to our communities' problems and more besides, but not at the expense of fundamental research. A balance must be struck, for in the need to protect original approaches in research, the University must ensure that the optimal environment is maintained, otherwise there will be no teachers of quality and nothing worthwhile teaching. . . .

We have recognised the need not only to apply our talents to the solutions of problems of a more universal nature, but also that we should give due attention to the problems of Africa. It would seem to me that university staff should be chosen solely on academic merit, that is, on the basis of scholarship. Any other method will result in mediocrity, or worse. It would seem to be shortsighted to indigenise the staff of African universities for the sake of indigenisation alone and such action would not be in the interests of students who seek tertiary education and inspiration in them. A university in Africa must accept the task of fostering and preserving the mutually enriching mixture of traditions and values which make up our African heritage and culture, and must set itself to helping to solve the pressing socioeconomic and other problems around it. Its graduates, educated in the universal ethos and trained in rationalism, will certainly be able to tackle these problems vigorously and must be encouraged to do so by the emphasis given to them by their teachers in course work, lectures, and tutorials, drawing not only from our universal experience but also from local factors, in which the teacher should be actively involved. In illustrating problems of labour and management, a study of our coal or gold mines is more relevant (and I use the word with care) at UCT than a study of the coal mines of South Wales, although South Wales cannot be ignored altogether—no rugby player would forgive us if we did so!

Role in Africa

In keeping with its role in Africa and its tradition of universality, UCT has rejected consistently and with deep conviction any consideration other than academic potential as a criterion for an individual to join its fellowship. In the words of Davie, a university must decide "who may teach, what may be taught, how it shall be taught and who may be admitted to study." This is a matter of high principle, emphasised over thirty years ago, and to which I fully subscribe. The wisdom of this approach is being underlined in pragmatic terms as we move further into the 1980s. . . .

South Africa does not have the financial or manpower resources to build and operate more and more universities. It is clear that it cannot rely upon the white population to provide enough graduates necessary for the full development of our nation. It is imperative that the maximum possible use be made of all the universities in South Africa to ensure that the most able of the matriculants of all ethnic groups are able to enjoy a university education and to provide the essential high-level manpower that we need. Pragmatic considerations alone underline the force of the request for the removal of the permit system under which South African blacks have to seek ministerial permission to attend this University. It is a system which is deeply resented, is insulting, and is unnecessary. It is also clear that it is not in the national interest. The Prime Minister has correctly called for a fundamental review of South African educational systems. I would hope that this will result in major reform, inter alia, ensuring a significantly greater expenditure on black education and the elimination of discrimination. But the backlog is so great that whatever solutions are found, emergency action is needed in the short and medium terms. For example, the full potential of radio and TV needs to be exploited in both secondary and tertiary education. The Open University in Great Britain is an illustration of what can be achieved as are the educational networks in the United States. The important university roles in continuing and adult education must be enlarged to help as well.

To Bridge the Gap

In trying to remedy the deficiencies of a segregated secondary school educational system in the United States, educationists have identified writing skills and mathematics as two key areas, and have set up remedial programmes especially in these subjects. I would advocate identifying children with potential in any school judged to be below average academically and to give them special upgrading courses in writing and mathematics, in the evenings, over weekends, and in the holidays, while they are still at school. Students underprepared for university, despite their symbols in school leaving examinations, will certainly need bridging programmes. Leading universities in the United States have found that even students from good schools have had such a need.

At UCT we have tried to identify underprepared students, and have instituted a special tutorial scheme where the tutors try to establish the problems of the students, be they personal, financial, lack of knowledge of study methods, etc., and try to help them overcome these difficulties.

I am saying that it is not enough merely to call for the opening of universities and the repeal of the Extension of University Education Act No. 45 of 1959, but that universities must also be prepared to make special efforts to ensure that as many students as possible succeed without any lowering of exit standards. The latter is a crucial point, and any departure from it strikes at the very heart of the University. We hope that the part-time degree programme in Arts and Science for school teachers, which was introduced in the University this year, will help to upgrade secondary education in the schools of the Western Cape; it illustrates another manner in which universities can try to help to solve this great problem. I would hope that we would get financial support to help us in these special efforts. Commerce and industry can help enormously by providing financial support in the academic and other areas. The state should seriously consider the introduction of two-year community colleges to bridge the gap between school and university for underprepared students.

Education is in crisis in this country, and the opening of the universities is but one of the solutions. It has been said that this might change our character. On the contrary, it will strengthen our universality. The mingling of minds, the free access to knowledge, and the educational strength of diversity in the student body have, in our own experience and in the experience of universities throughout the Western world, proved to be sources of enrichment and strength. The character of a university is determined by scholarship and not by ethnicity. I might add that what is true of a university is true for society in general. Differences between peoples should be used to enhance their contributions to society by bringing them together in a spirit of mutual respect.

It is strange, to say the least, that just as the black staff in the hospital kitchen at Groote Schuur Hospital can live on the premises but *not* the black nurses, so in universities black staff in Residences are allowed to live on the campus, but *not* black students. The problems which the black students have with regard to adequate housing are enormous. Sanity and goodwill must prevail here.

It should be remembered that a university must never propound a particular political ideology or seek to support a political party. Universities which have followed this course have lost their objectivity and rationality, indeed, their right to exist as universities. When politics impinge on the autonomy of the university, when ideology tries to inhibit scholarship, it is the university's duty to respond, and to respond vigorously. A nation would be ill-served by a university which did not do so.

Communication is essential for scholarship. Situated as we are, at the tip of Africa, our staff need to maintain close contact with scholars elsewhere in the world, and the University's Study and Research, Special, and Contact Leaves make this possible.

Unworthy of Cultured Men

I am troubled by attempts by some to impose an academic boycott on this country's universities. This would seem to me to be the negation of everything that a university holds dear. Surely the exchange of ideas and the mutual search for truth can only help to solve problems in a reasonable manner, whereas isolation can only aggravate and increase the risk of unacceptable solutions. I do not believe that any political consideration should be put as a hindrance to the advance of knowledge or to the education of the young.

I am reminded of the example of Einstein who was threatened together with his fellow Germans with an academic boycott after World War I. The nuclear physicists tried to make an exception in his case but Einstein would have none of it. Knowing that his colleagues were to be barred, because they were German nationals, from the fourth Solvay Congress on Physics, Einstein declined even to receive an invitation. He said to Madame Curie, "It is unworthy of cultured men to treat one another in that type of superficial way, as though they were members of the common herd, being led by mass suggestion." It is surely incredible for the scientific world to have held a congress on physics in the 1920s without Germans like Max Planck. Individuals may decline to associate with other groups because the values that such other groups hold are repugnant to them. That is a personal choice, but it is quite another matter when organisations try to interfere with the movement of scholars. Academic boycotts are certainly not in the interests of the furtherance of knowledge or the search for truth.

Communication between scholars implies access to source material, and the Publications Act and Internal Security Act in the Republic create major difficulties in this regard. A large number of publications may not be held even for possession by the universities, so they are totally inaccessible. Others may be held for possession, but access to them is so rigidly controlled that not a single application to consult these books and publications has been received at the library at UCT over the past 12 months. The net result of this censorship is that a subject like communism, a clear and serious threat to western civilisation, cannot be adequately studied as archival resources of key material are fragmentary to say the least. If scholars cannot be informed on communism and cannot enter into a debate on Marxism, how can counter arguments be developed? How can the myths be exposed? In the presence of censorship, how can we reach the truth? In a decision of the Publications Appeal Board handed down on 26 September 1979, it is reported that "The Appeal Board has consulted with the librarians of the Pretoria University, UNISA, the State Library, Pretoria, and Mr. C. J. van der Merwe, M.A., Senior Lecturer in Political Science and Chairman of the Department of Political Science at the Randse Afrikaanse Universiteit. The Appeal Board invited these gentlemen to a discussion of the matter and also two members of the Security Police who deal with undesirable publications. The unanimous view of all these gentlemen was that the restrictions imposed in respect of Section 9 (3) prohibitions are so severe that they defeat the purpose they seek to serve. Important sources of political knowledge are therefore lost to students— not because students are refused access to it, but because of the frustration caused to them by the "red tape" and especially the delay in gaining access. A student in the course of research finds the delay caused by applying for permission such that he avoids such books or resorts to inferior substitutes. In the field of political research this can have serious consequences. Our intelligentsia cannot properly qualify themselves." Need more be said?

Scholarship is also damaged by any infringement on the freedom of speech or association of individuals. Acts against members of the university community, staff and students alike, which silence them, make their publications, scholarly or otherwise, prohibited in this country, and prevent them from teaching or doing their research without their being charged with, or found guilty of, any crime, are totally unacceptable, and threaten every scholar and citizen in this country. There can be no freedom to explore the truth in a society which has such laws on its statute books, and it is freedom, not licence, that the University seeks. The right to seek the truth to the full, without fear or favour, is what a university is all about. Bannings and arbitrary arrests without habeas corpus strike at the heart of a university and of civilization itself. . . .

Faith in Students

The SRC is an elected body representing the students. Despite the impression given by some newspaper reports, the record of the SRC at UCT is a very good one. If the members of the SRC never did anything controversial, if we always found ourselves in agreement with the student leadership, would they be acting as we did, or as our parents did, as students? I very much doubt it. I don't believe that we would want it to be so.

Students are correct to demand the right to express themselves. When the National Union of South African Students (NUSAS) calls for equal rights for all people, we should applaud them, and encourage them to help South Africans to find peaceful solutions to our many problems. It should not surprise us if we are at one time or another in disagreement with various student bodies. I have great faith in our students, and salute their idealism and courage.

[Autonomy of Universities]

In the United Kingdom and in the United States of America, universities are concerned about their relationship to government. In Britain the University Grants Committee is placed between the Department of Education and Science and the Universities, and allocates funds to them. There is concern to ensure that the University Grants Committee retains its independence and that the autonomy of the universities is protected. In the United States the encroachment of the Federal Government on universities is also feared, particularly the accountability of the universities for funds which can be under threat if certain Federal demands are not met. In this country, the universities receive some 80 percent of their funds from the State, and it is to the great credit of the government that these funds, with minor exceptions, once given to the universities, are not earmarked in any way, but the expenditure is left to the discretion of the universities themselves. This autonomy of the universities is treasured in this country, and I believe that in this respect we are in a much more favourable position than some of the universities in Europe or elsewhere in the world. . . .

I have dealt at some length with contemporary issues and problems facing this and other universities, but it would be quite wrong for me not to emphasise the sense of excitement and adventure that permeates the University of Cape Town. It springs from its scholars and its students, from its Council and its Senate, from all its constituent parts, from people, and not from buildings. It is the quality of the people that matters. The courageous Czech philosopher, Julius Tomin, a member of the Charter 77 movement, held seminars in his home in Prague despite harassment by the Security Police. The Oxford philosophers individually joined these seminars and the lounge of his home became a university. It is the quality of scholarship that is vital. . . .

DOCUMENT X:

Programs to Increase Black Enrollment at the University of Cape Town (1980)

*In a memorandum of November 6, 1980, excerpts of which fol-
low, the administration of the University of Cape Town (UCT)
described special programs for which it would welcome American or other external support. Despite the laws setting racial
criteria for admissions, UCT has continued to apply academic
criteria alone. And in the increasing number of cases in which
the government has granted individual permits, qualified
blacks have been admitted. Black enrollment at UCT is expected to rise rapidly in the years just ahead.*

Assisted University Places

What are the obstacles (other than the need to obtain a permit,
which may be and often is refused) that face black students or
that prevent blacks from enrolling or graduating if they want to
attend a so-called "white" university (a term that universities like
Cape Town and Witwatersrand have never accepted)? Essentially these are

□ many black students are underprepared, coming from inadequate and inferior school systems;

□ most black students are unable to pay tuition fees and have difficulty in finding and paying for accommodation; transport from black living areas is a further problem;

□ many black students do not see clear avenues to employment after graduation.

PROGRAMMES FOR UNDERPREPARED STUDENTS

Those "white" universities with significant numbers of black students—the Witwatersrand, Cape Town and Natal—have in the past two years (1979–1980) embarked upon programmes for providing academic support to underprepared students from disadvantaged academic backgrounds. These programmes are on a small scale, dictated by the limited funding available, nearly all of which has come from donors or charitable organisations. No government funding is available for these programmes, [but] institutions are unlikely to be able to meet the[se] challenges without significant support from corporations, foundations, and eventually government.

The Republic has no equivalent of the U.S. community colleges. A school leaver seeking a place in higher education will opt either for a university place or for technical training at one of the Technikons. At the end of this decade the number of black school leavers with matriculation (the minimum qualification for admission to a university) will exceed 35,000 (1978: less than 7,000). The predicted figure for whites is 30,000 (1978: 22,500). In 1978 blacks accounted for less than 20 percent of country-wide residential university enrollment. The standard of schooling for blacks is not going to improve overnight, and many in South Africa would see the need for community college-type institutions at which school leavers who cannot gain admission to university places would enroll for bridging programmes designed to equip them for university. An ambitious and large-scale project would be to found such institutions in the major centres of Johannesburg, Cape Town, Durban, and Port Elizabeth.

FINANCING BLACK STUDY AT UNIVERSITY

A black student wishing to enroll at the University of Cape Town would be required to find between $2,000 and $2,500 each year in order to meet tuition fees, accommodation, and transport costs. This University, like others such as the Witwatersrand (where costs are of the same order), is able to help some students from the bursary and loan funds at its disposal, funds which are awarded on the basis of scholastic merit and financial need, but is not going to be able to help the significant numbers of blacks which it hopes to enroll in the next ten years.

One way it hopes to meet this challenge is by devising a *Cadet Scheme*. Essentially this is intended to be a partnership between the university and a prospective employer. The university and the sponsor would recruit black students satisfying the university's admission criteria; the student would enroll at the university which would ensure that he had access to academic support programmes, and the sponsor would pay tuition and living costs. Furthermore, the sponsor would be expected to offer the student a job on graduation or, in other cases might require the student to take a job in the corporation on graduation for a period not longer than the period during which he received support.

It needs to be stressed that tuition and living expenses of between $2,000 and $2,500 per year are outside the means of the overwhelming majority of blacks, whose families usually have no capital, own no land, and have a total annual disposable income considerably less than this amount. If access to higher education is to have any meaning for them, financial support is going to be essential. Anybody who has the resources to do so can make a contribution in this area. In particular, all employers who are in fact committed to making the best use of the human resources of the country should look at it seriously.

Teacher Training [and Assistance] Programmes

The lack of adequately trained teachers is likely to remain one of the Republic's major educational problems. Every conceivable strategy will have to be used to meet this. In the first place, the unqualified and underqualified teachers in the black schools need assistance and one way in which this is being tackled is illustrated by the part-time degree programme which the University of Cape Town is hoping to offer for the first time in 1981. This is an expensive after-hours programme aimed specifically at the unqualified teachers in service in the black schools in the Cape. Initiatives of this sort deserve support and could produce significant results.

Schools, in particular high schools, in the black community are notoriously short of rudimentary teaching aids. Projects, such as the Science Education Project (SEP), which started in the Eastern Cape and which has been used with impressive results in Soweto, have been started to try to overcome the lack of laboratory facilities in these schools using simple, inexpensive kits and specially prepared teaching and learning materials, making science education more meaningful in schools where, for example, classrooms do not have electricity points or running water. Projects of this sort, and innovative work and research which shows promise of developing this sort of project, need support.

[In the same memorandum, the administration set forth the results of its efforts to diversify its student body.]

The University's policies on enrollment of students irrespective of race are very often frustrated by government legislation. The

TABLE 1
Enrollment Figures for 1980

| | Undergraduates | | Graduate Students | | |
	Male	Female	Male	Female	Total
White	4,620	2,774	1,339	599	9,332
Coloured	463	284	81	20	848
Asian	152	53	17	8	230
Chinese	20	4	1	–	25
Black (African)	29	15	19	8	71
TOTAL	5,284	3,130	1,457	635	10,506

Extension of University Education Act of 1959 requires every person who is not classified by law as white, who has been accepted by the University for admission as a student, to obtain the authority of a Minister of State before he or she may enroll as a student. The University vigorously opposed the introduction of this measure and remains resolutely opposed to it. In spite of this measure, the University has continued to accept applications on merit and the number and proportion of enrolled students who are not classified white continues to grow. This is evidenced by the fact that the 1980 enrollment, university-wide, included slightly more than 11 percent blacks (the term "black" includes Africans, so-called Coloureds, Asians, and Chinese) while the proportion of freshmen was 17.8 percent.

The Origins and Goals of the Rand Afrikaans University (1981)

In its official brochure, Prospectus 1981, *RAU provides a description of its mission as a white, ethnic university. Endowed with imposing architecture and an automated library, the university combines traditional ethnic particularism with modern pedagogy and the latest in instructional technology.*

Major Goals of the RAU

When the RAU was established in 1967, it had to justify its entry into a rather crowded scene, since South Africa was then already generously served by sixteen universities and more than thirty colleges offering tertiary education in professional fields such as teacher training, advanced technology, nursing, and agriculture.

The primary aim of the new University was to raise educational standards and opportunities for the large concentration of Afrikaans-speaking Whites living on the Witwatersrand. In fact, after twelve years the RAU had a student population of 4,804 in 1980, yet its rapid growth rate has not affected that of the three existing neighbouring universities, thus establishing its claim of drawing underutilized brain potential to higher education.

The second aim of the new University has been to focus its teaching and research on the needs and challenges of the big city, as the new environment within which the formerly rural Afrikaner people have had to shape their future.

A third major goal the new University, with its unique opportunity for educational and instructional innovation, set itself was the rationalization and modernization of its programmes and especially its methods of instruction. . . .

□ *Study guides.* For each course students are provided with a free set of basic notes, enabling them to come to lectures better prepared.

□ The RAU has considerably less time devoted to lectures in each course than the average at other universities, with the result that students have more time available for self-study and work in the library.

□ *Group classes.* Larger lecture groups in all courses are broken up into two-weekly group or tutorial classes of not more than 20 students per group. Every student receives the benefit of individual attention, even in courses with large student numbers.

□ *The semester system.* With a few exceptions, all subjects are offered in semester [rather than year-long] courses. Because each semester is examined separately, the student is required to give an account of himself quite early in the year. This compels a student to commence studying seriously earlier in the year and to maintain a sustained effort.

□ *Continuous testing.* A student's final mark is based not only on a single semester or year examination, but also on tests and assignments set during the term.

This requires continuous study from the outset, but it also protects the student against examination "mishaps." Testing starts early in each semester so that remedial work can commence as soon as possible.

□ *Educational media.* A language laboratory, overhead projectors, film and slide projectors, and tape recorders are integrated into the teaching process.

The above are a few of a series of fruitful measures aimed at more effective teaching.

Further emphasis on the individual appears from such measures as the provision of residences for not more than 250 students per "house," designed to stimulate the growth of subgroups; attractive day residence facilities are provided for commuting students spending many hours on the campus; a lively competitive spirit among the residences in sport, cultural performances, and even in the academic sphere is fostered; a team of advisors drawn from senior students is provided, each advisor aiding six to eight first-year students, and an academic and personal Academic Advice Bureau with a staff of educationists and psychologists provides an essential service. A consultative committee between Senate and the Students' Council, and student representation on Senate committees of direct interest to them, ensure frequent and effective communication between the student and academic leadership.

A gratifying result especially of the educational innovation of the RAU has been the fact that in spite of the regional character reflected by its name (Rand Afrikaans University), it soon established a national reputation and attracted up to a third of its student body from outside the Witwatersrand, its immediate area of recruitment, some students coming from other Transvaal regions but many hailing from other provinces and even from neighbouring countries.

Teaching Staff

□ The RAU has a dynamic, youthful staff with training and experience at all South African universities and at leading universities of the Western world.

□ The RAU conducts an extensive programme of annual international exchanges, including overseas research visits by staff members and arrangements for visiting professors from abroad.

□ Regular discussions, seminars, and conferences are organized in order to stimulate local and national contact with other universities, and also interaction between the professors, and commerce and industry.

□ Regular staff symposia on university teaching and in research areas are conducted in order to keep academic activities at an optimum level.

Spirit and Character

In terms of the preamble to the Act on the Rand Afrikaans University, the University is "Afrikaans in spirit and character" and will "maintain the principles set out in the preamble to the Constitution of the Republic." Among others these principles express "humble submission to the Almighty God, who controls the destinies of nations and the history of peoples."

Students of all religious denominations are welcome to register (and a considerable percentage of various denominations and language groups do register) at the RAU, although, as one would expect, the Protestant character of its Afrikaans-speaking students predominates.

The Inaugural Address of Dr. Mike de Vries, Rector of the University of Stellenbosch (1979)

Stellenbosch projects itself into the future with a confidence conveyed by its fundraising brochure: Stellenbosch 2000: An Investment in Manpower and Leaders for the Future. *When read alongside that of Stuart Saunders' of the neighboring University of Cape Town, Rector Mike de Vries' (September 7, 1979) inaugural address is notable for its communal focus and social serenity. The social ferment of the urban university seems but a distant, muffled rumble.*

Tonight I would like to address myself to the theme: a university for the South Africa of the future.

In order to appraise the needs and challenges of the future, it is well also to look back at the past and try to understand how and where the roots of this tree, the University of Stellenbosch, which has been with us for so long, are really anchored.

A great deal can be said about the beginnings of higher education at Stellenbosch, the Stellenbosch Gymnasium (1866), and the Victoria College (1887), and much has already been written, but nowhere are the roots of the tree and the soil in which it grows more clearly outlined than in the period directly before the development of this University as an independent academic establishment in 1918. The struggle against a single "examining" university in Cape Town, which started as long ago as the last years of the previous century, was at its fiercest just after the birth of Union. Various draft laws were opposed and in 1913 a memorandum, compiled by Dr. D. F. Malan, Mr. J. G. van der Horst and Prof. Moorrees, was introduced in which among other things the following appeared:

> Stellenbosch is the place where the Afrikaner nation can best realise its ideals and from where it can exert the greatest influence on South Africa. It would be the best fulfilment the nation has yet found of a deeply felt need. *It stands for an idea!* To the nation it has therefore become not a mere educational institution, but also a symbol and the guarantee of its own vigorous, growing national life seeking to express itself. (Translated from the Dutch.)

There is not enough time to fully analyse this phrase, but it is clear that the tree had its origin within the Afrikaner society— rooted in the soil of South Africa. As in nature, the fruit will also bear the stamp of the tree and the soil. Therefore the tree and its fruit, the University and its people, have always been—like the Afrikaner society—conservative of nature, with a religious character and a definite South African patriotism.

The period in which this plea for recognition was made, and during which the words, "Stellenbosch stands for an idea," were first mooted, as well as the following years, were extremely difficult ones for South Africa, standing as she did on the threshold of her industrial development. World War One, the Rebellion, strikes and riots, as well as the depression, brought doubts and heralded an uncertain future. In religious circles, in education, agriculture, the legal profession, industry, and politics, however, leaders came to the fore—bearing the stamp of the tree at Stellenbosch. Men of quality, men with initiative, levelheaded men of judgement and conduct, served unselfishly and thus helped to bridge the dark years. Academic excellence is without doubt one of the cornerstones on which every university is built, but the Stellenbosch idea, formulated so long ago, has extended much further than merely establishing an intellectual elite.

Service to the community, pioneering work and renewal, and producing people who could adapt to the times and its challenges were equally part of this idea.

This historical role of Stellenbosch as a leading and renewing force on the South African scene places especially difficult responsibilities on the University. Of course there is the temptation, so often unconscious and therefore all the more dangerous, to rest on one's laurels and to believe that what has been achieved in the past is also our historical and obvious heritage. Much rather it is the responsibility of this University to make its historical heritage come *true* again and again.

As so often in the past, and particularly in the period to which I referred, South Africa once again faces an uncertain future. Many people are inclined to see the eighties as one grey cloud bristling with dark question marks, impenetrable even through the light of faith. We are rooted at the southern tip of a continent where the instability of a post-colonial era continues to build up. South Africa herself is decried by her critics, also in Western circles, as a kind of anachronism which cannot survive in its present form.

Internally our problems are legion. A population growth of 76 percent is predicted for the following twenty-one years, which, inter alia, will mean

☐ 1.2 million people needing housing annually; that is somewhat more than the present population of greater Cape Town— a city per year!

☐ the creation of six hundred new job opportunities per day, and by the year 2000 about 1,000 new job opportunities per day;

☐ that whereas at the moment we have an annual growth rate of hardly 3.6 percent, the figure should actually be between 5.5 percent and 6.0 percent if unemployment is to be effectively combatted;

☐ that internal saving will have to increase drastically and that more labour-intensive methods will have to be employed;

☐ that the ratio between the entrepreneurs and the executive group of the population who create the work opportunities will have to go up in relation to the skilled, semi-skilled, and un-skilled groups. At present this ratio is decreasing (1 to 52 in 1978, to a predicted 1 to 76 in 2000) with resultant slower growth and its inevitable results;

□ that training and schooling should be the highest priorities. This alone is a gigantic task if one considers that it is calculated that seven schools per day will have to be built merely for pupils of our black population group.

Prophets of doom could play more and more little games with figures, and we need not even look further than the Western Cape where our University is situated and where we should give urgent attention and assistance.

What a mighty challenge! Because of its heterogeneous population, the Republic of South Africa, unlike other Western countries, cannot be regarded as a developed country. We must realise that we are a developed as well as an underdeveloped country and that we cannot apply the standards of the former only. In a certain sense, one may say that the Republic of South Africa is a reflection of both the "First World" and the "Third World"—a pocketbook edition of all the problems of developed, semideveloped and underdeveloped societies, or a microcosmos of the macrocosmos!

The subcontinent of which we are part is in motion and in our South African society too we have entered a phase of rapid change on a wide variety of terrains. The placid pace of a "platteland" culture has made way for a dynamic process of urbanisation, continued modernisation, and political awakening. In the previous century we had the Great Trek when the vast spaces of South Africa were explored and occupied. Today we have a different kind of Great Trek—the trek of the spirit of man to reconnoitre and occupy a new period in time.

If we as a university accept this challenge, if we want to be of service in the period ahead of our country, and if we want to help in leading the new Trek, then it is right and necessary to retain our historic perspective and to define clearly the points of departure for the forward journey. I have already referred to the roots of this tree and the soil in which they are anchored. As a point of departure I stress this once again. The Afrikaner community always has been and always shall be the lifeblood of the University of Stellenbosch; and, as in the past and precisely because of its *Afrikaans character*, our University must be at the service of South Africa and its people as a whole. It is also necessary—imperative in this period—to strive for an understanding of ourselves in future perspective—not so much to try and ascertain what the future will be, but to try and prevent precisely those things for which we do not want to accept responsibility and which we do not desire, from dominating the years to come.

What do we want then? Where lies our contribution? What are our spheres of service?

The quality and scope of university education form one of the most important cornerstones of the quality of life that can be brought about in a developing society such as ours.

It is plain fact that economic as well as technological and political development cannot succeed without broadly conceived community development. In other words the economic structures to be developed and the political life-patterns to be created cannot function successfully if the community within which they operate does not maintain a high level of culture in the matter of responsibility, of values, of moral codes, and of general mental attitudes. Particularly in this area I see one of the future tasks of this University.

Secondly, great stress is usually laid on the teaching and research functions of a university, on the gathering of knowledge and the imparting of new knowledge, with less emphasis on its application. The University must never, as regards these three facets, advance excuses if, in the academic sphere, it should drop below internationally recognised levels. This simply should not happen. In its traditional functions of teaching, research, and application of knowledge our University must therefore

□ continuously check whether our teaching techniques still meet the demands of the times. What was effective formerly, is not necessarily so now. We will, because of the enormous quantity of knowledge, have to adjust ourselves to teach students to master new knowledge themselves. A student who has not been taught how to assimilate new knowledge independently is being let down by his lecturers. Postgraduate training will have to be sought after purposefully, because in most avenues today a first degree alone is insufficient to meet the demands of the future and amounts to a mere scratching of the surface;

□ continuously account to ourselves as to whether our education is still relevant. Does it still relate to the realities of the eighties? Educational stagnation is one of the very ways to smother the development of leadership! The painful process of self-criticism and self-correction must be applied continuously in our own ranks. "Do not look outside for what is lacking inside," said Langenhoven;

□ continuously endeavour to conduct and maintain academic dialogue within our University either in the faculties, in the Senate, by way of "think tanks" between the various disciplines, or between lecturers and students, or among students themselves;

□ ensure that research is stimulated and of a high standard; otherwise intellectual brain hardening will set in and the University will become a museum of obsolete knowledge;

□ carefully establish research priorities and synchronise them with the needs of the community, not only for financial reasons, but especially because a developing society can in no way afford the luxury of irrelevant research. We will have to apply our minds to a comprehensive research policy which will show the way research should follow and make provision for coordinated interdisciplinary research projects;

□ ensure that our academics maintain contact with practice and are not only involved in investigative roles, but also in the application of their recommendations;

□ in the words of Genesis 2, verse 15, this "Garden of Eden . . . must be *cultivated* and *guarded*," not only within the academic assignment of cultivation that we envisage for a university, but also as a universal cultural imperative.

But then, its traditional functions, however well pursued, are not the only ones facing the University if it truly wants to serve future society.

A fourth basic function, namely the general shaping of responsible human existence, is equally important. The University of Stellenbosch has in the past claimed that it did not only concern itself with the intellectual development of its students. That is why student societies, residence organisation, large-scale participation in team sports, development of healthy recreative sport, close integration with church activities, community service through USKOR, the Mission Week and even the song festival, form such a typical part of student life at Stellenbosch. That is why my predecessor, Prof. J. N. de Villiers, actively strove for student participation and consultation at various levels of decision-making at our University. All this denotes a wider development of being and the acceptance of responsibility.

This moulding function of the University is essential to community development. Our teaching too must be organised to produce responsible and complete personalities for the society we serve. If we want to serve we must realise

☐ that the creation of responsible and committed citizenship is essential to the sound working of democracy;

☐ that we shall have to generate sensitivity to basic civilized values, not only within our own student body, but also throughout South African society. Disregard in this respect has had a superficialising and paralysing influence in the "First World" during recent years, and for a developing country this could be fatal;

☐ that we as a University must take the lead in regard to basic civilized values, as this will decide the issue during the eighties. It is an ideal that the University of Stellenbosch should be a central nervous system for South Africa and all its peoples, and that we should, without sacrificing our Afrikaans character, explore ways of sharing with other population groups that which could enrich our common future;

□ that we, true to our roots and the soil in which we are anchored, must play a role during the eighties in cultivating patriotism and a common loyalty to the Republic of South Africa. At staff as well as student level there must be contact and communication with community leaders of all population groups to further mutual understanding;

□ that value awareness on the part of the University must be sharpened among its students and within the community. This will mean responsible decision-making, having regard to future tendencies as well as expressing our commitment to help in deciding the quality of life desired.

The four functions of a university for the future which I have mentioned, lead to a fifth. These four functions comprise the university as a centre of service, as a centre of selection and discrimination, as an assembly line, and as a central nervous system of culture.

The fifth function, however, is that of a radar network where future trends in society—economic, social and political—can be scanned and processed so that the aircraft can be brought safely to reality (ground). We must ever be ahead of the community and—even if they should criticise us—lead them with honest arguments. In this we, as the University, must be prepared as in the past—yes, even more strongly than in the past—to move outward from the pampered tranquility of a three-hundred-year-old Boland town. Our radar rays must encompass the total South African community.

We have a proud past; I see a future in which we still stand for an idea. I see a future where we would be prepared to think more broadly than the traditional boundaries, where we will shake off standardisation that can only lead to decline, where we are ready for differentiation and growth, and for the realisation that here at the southernmost tip of the continent of Africa there are greater challenges to meet than in any other place in the world. I see a University poised to be the architect instead of the slave of change; poised to span the traditional boundaries, and with an unshakeable faith in the future of our fatherland. I see a University investing in human material—the best on the academic level—rather than in land and buildings. I see a University initiating renewal with balanced judgement and conduct. I also see a University spreading the message of a stable future, of faith, of hope, backed by balanced thinking and willing to be in the forefront to pioneer and traverse the uncharted paths of the future. I see a University putting itself at the service of our Afrikaner community, the Western Cape or, if our services are needed, the Transkei, Ciskei or Bophuthatswana—the entire Southern Africa. I see a University putting itself at the service of the community through its first-rate expertise.

Where I have tried to gather guidelines from the past for the future, my predominant message is one of faith in Him who determines the future for us all, faith in the people of South Africa who will find and understand one another, and also faith that the contribution of each one of us will mean something. It is not necessary to look for challenges further afield—they are here in our midst!

I want to give the assurance that we as University still stand for an idea—the idea of service, of the acceptance of the above-mentioned challenges and a firm faith that together we shall safeguard our future; as well as an idea that academic merits and first-rate expertise will—and must—play a role in the safeguarding of our common future.

Toward a Mission for the African University in South Africa (1981)

In September 1981, Rector A. C. Nkabinde of the University of Zululand convened a symposium of South African educators at Empangeni to discuss appropriate goals for an African university. At the conclusion of the Symposium on the Definition of Goals, consensus was reached on the following principles.

1. A university must be open to all qualified persons who wish to enroll as students.

2. A university must be committed to the pursuit of knowledge and truth for the amelioration of the lot of the members of society.

3. A university is an instrument for the reconstruction of society. It is an instrument of change.

4. A university must retain the universality of human experience and also reflect the nature of the environment in which it operates.

A university must have relevance to its task in the community.

5. Students must play a meaningful rôle in the community.

6. There is need for the investigation of appropriate technology in a Third World university.

7. A university on African soil has something to contribute to the sum total of knowledge. Consequently, there is need for a pervasive study of African languages and literature, history, economics, law, religion, customs, and traditions, etc.

8. The university can only play a meaningful rôle in its service to the community if it knows the needs and problems of society. A research institute is, therefore, a very high priority. Without such an institute the university can never hope to know and understand the problems confronting it.

A strong research institute would have a two-pronged purpose, viz. to collect, analyse, collate and preserve information on the one hand and be a source of teaching material on the other.

9. A university must train its students to think independently.

10. The primary purpose of a university is to train people for vocations.

The training of people for vocations should not be construed as a contradiction of a university's aim to promote academic excellence.

11. A university must have a clearly defined staffing policy.

12. A university must radiate a spirit of liberty to the teachers and students.

The freedom to think, to probe, to question, and to engage in academic discourse is fundamental.

13. A university must be creative.

[In an effort to implement these principles, for which purposes he would welcome foreign assistance, Nkabinde mandated the Rector's Committee on Current Issues to make specific recommendations on the following:

1. The basis on which a Research Institute should be established and what fields of knowledge it should encompass.

2. How students can "play a meaningful role in the University."

3. What the University's faculty recruitment policy should be.

4. The fields in which the University of Zululand can have the most impact in its contribution "to the sum total of knowledge with minimum effort and delay."

5. How the University can fulfill its goal of "teaching students to think independently."

6. How the University can be made "relevant to the community."]

DOCUMENT XIV:

The University and Development in Transkei (1981)

In the first issue of the Transkei Development Review, *Wolfgang H. Thomas describes the goals of the Institute for Management and Development Studies (IMDS) and the intended role of the journal. The journal's overview of a 1981 conference on development issues in Transkei is also included. The rural poverty of Transkei and other African homelands is acute and pervasive. Thus the ability of homeland universities to lead an assault on the problems of rural development assumes great importance.*

THE IMDS AND THE *TRANSKEI DEVELOPMENT REVIEW*
WOLFGANG H. THOMAS

Since 1977 the University of Transkei [Unitra] has been committed to playing a significant role in assisting the process of socioeconomic development in southern Africa, with particular emphasis on the Transkei region. Initially the focus fell on business-oriented training with the Transkei Institute for Entrepreneurship and Management (TIEM) being established in coop-

eration with the Graduate School of Business of the University
of Stellenbosch. From the beginning it was envisaged that this
Institute would eventually be taken over by Unitra and that its
activities would be broadened to include development-oriented
applied research, training, and assistance in the task of rural
development. This was effected during 1980 when the Institute
for Management and Development Studies (IMDS) was established as an autonomous body within the University's Faculty of
Economic Sciences.

The task of the new Institute is set out as follows:

> It is to engage in those development-oriented activities which are
> linked to the training and research functions of the Faculty—and
> related disciplines in other faculties—but which are not directly
> part of its normal activities. Initially the emphasis will fall on the
> training function and the undertaking of applied research into
> problems of development, with special emphasis being given to
> issues of rural and agricultural development in the southern Af-
> rican context. It is also envisaged to initiate interdisciplinary pilot
> projects related to the particular socioeconomic development
> needs of the Transkei region.

To finance its activities the Institute is largely dependent on outside sponsorship and commissioned research.

In its Training Division the Institute will be concerned with
the organisation of conferences, workshops, day seminars, and
shorter courses related to in-service training of the public as well
as the private sector. The conference on "Development Issues"
was the first major activity of the Institute's Training Division.
In the sphere of business training TIEM is about to merge with
IMDS, and in the sphere of public sector training close cooperation with the Public Service Commission is foreseen. With respect to rural development the Institute will concentrate on the
propagation of the integrated rural development approach and
on practical assistance in the planning, implementation, monitoring, and training relevant to grassroots rural development.
The Research Division will be concerned with the collection,
dissemination, [and] interpretation of data on Transkeian development and also the detailed investigation of specific development problems.

For the dissemination of research findings and as a basis for the wider discussion of development issues the Institute has launched the (quarterly) *Transkei Development Review*. Individual issues will usually focus on a central theme, and contain conference or workshop papers or commissioned articles. In addition it is intended, as the basis for a possible future Transkei Statistical Bulletin, to include a collection of regularly updated statistical series in the *Review*. In addition individual (working) papers, relevant addresses or shorter research reports will be released as IMDS Fact Papers or IMDS Discussion Papers. Their particular role should be to stimulate thinking, policy formulation and action relevant to the socioeconomic development of Transkei as an integral part of southern Africa.

This first issue of the *TDR* is fully taken up by papers delivered at the March conference on "Development Issues in Transkei."

DEVELOPMENT ISSUES IN TRANSKEI: A CONFERENCE OVERVIEW

Background

Organised jointly by the Institute for Management and Development Studies, the Transkei Public Service Commission, the National Planning Commission, and by individuals from the University of Natal, this conference was seen by participants as

□ the first major step in a broad programme of in-service training focused on government officials;

□ the first opportunity for the newly created Institute for Management and Development Studies to forge closer links between academics and civil servants;

□ help[ing to] draw attention to some of the issues underlying the forthcoming Five-Year Plan and to the need for an ongoing debate on such issues.

The focus at the conference was primarily on the public sector, but nevertheless various issues related to the involvement in development of private enterprise were also raised and will be followed up in mid-May 1981 by a one-day conference arranged in collaboration with a number of Transkeian Chambers of Commerce.

While the conference was structured so as to place particular emphasis on rural development, attention was also paid to a fairly broad spectrum of other development issues. . . . The task of this overview is to highlight some of the underlying themes of the conference and certain more significant controversies and conclusions.

Development Issues

The Chief Economic Adviser to the Transkei Government, Prof. G. G. van Beers, outlined certain basic dilemmas—for example, that of high population growth rates—facing Third World countries such as Transkei. For him the challenge lay in finding a new equilibrium between legitimate needs, available resources, and the restraints imposed by the environment.

[In] the three days of addresses and discussions on Transkei's "continuing state of underdevelopment," the term "development" was taken to refer to two distinct concepts, viz. that of providing for the satisfaction of people's basic needs and that of providing for human development. As regards the former, "development means being freed from basic material wants such as the next meal, adequate shelter and clothing, water for washing and drinking, etc." The human development concept, on the other hand, suggests that people in general should have command over the provision and distribution of goods and services, and that the choices available to them should increase over time.

Transkei's development dilemma can be summarised [as follows]:

□ Over 90 percent of Transkei's resident population still lives in the rural areas where basic infrastructure and facilities such as electric lighting and piped water for domestic use are lacking;

☐ commercial and communication services are limited largely to isolated trading stores, post offices, and an inadequate telephone network;

☐ community facilities such as hospitals, clinics, and agricultural extension services are often widely scattered and inadequately equipped and staffed;

☐ local wage employment covers only about 15 percent of the Transkeian labour force and is mostly restricted to the two larger towns of Butterworth and Umtata;

☐ the number of Transkeian migrant workers employed outside the country has increased over recent years, reaching a current level of almost 70 percent of all able-bodied men;

☐ both the civil service and the few larger commercial and industrial enterprises are experiencing a critical shortage of adequately skilled and experienced workers;

☐ the prevailing attitude among rural people is one of apathy and suspicion, a direct consequence of decades of exclusion from effective decision-making;

☐ as a result of its failure to obtain international recognition Transkei, though a Least Developed Country (LDC), cannot rely on the normal level and diversity of foreign aid and expertise regarded as appropriate for other LDCs.

In conclusion and in contrast to much of the debate amongst other participants it may be worth [reiterating that] Transkei's underdevelopment should be regarded as a function of South Africa's unequal development rather than merely as one instance of Third World underdevelopment. Naturally, this also implies that attempts to "solve" Transkei's development problems will have little chance of success unless they take account of the broader development pattern.

The Role and Function of Planning

The gravity of many of the development issues has during the past few years given development planning and the search for appropriate development strategies increasing weight.

In order to avoid the imbalances of development on a crisis-management basis it is necessary for planning to be systematic and coherent. Seen from this perspective, development planning is primarily a management tool for policy-makers. Effective development planning calls therefore for the close integration of the development efforts of physical and economic planners, government departments, and national, regional, district, and village authorities. Unless the requisite administrative skills and capabilities are available, plans, however comprehensive or ambitious, cannot be converted into reality. In Transkei this has proven to be one of the most significant bottlenecks.

Motivation for Effective Development

An important concern underlying much of the discussion throughout the conference related to the motivation of individuals—peasants and workers as well as the middle and upper strata, civil servants, and politicians—in the struggle for higher living standards and more dynamic development. [Some] placed considerable emphasis on the moral conviction and dedication of individuals. They portrayed the "human factor" as the central force in the whole development process. Individuals, particularly those in power, would have to accept their responsibilities, "face up to the realities of the situation," and recognise that progress depends on "ability and performance."

Others preferred to focus on structural constraints on development, both within Transkei itself and in its relationship to South Africa. Declaring that while he did not condone it the existence of corruption did not amaze him, Prof. Thomas argued that there were concrete causes underlying both corruption and the apparent lack of competence and responsibility in government.

While these two apparently opposed approaches fueled a lively and at times heated debate, it would be wrong to assume that they are mutually exclusive. It is surely as mistaken to deny all individual responsibility as it would be to fail to investigate the structural factors underlying administrative and governmental shortcomings. The low salaries paid middle-echelon civil servants encourage them to look for supplementary sources of income, while poor education and training, a high staff turnover, and lack of competition for posts as well as a long-standing relationship of dependency vis-à-vis South Africa lead to uncertainty and a lack of initiative in the execution of functions. The shortage of senior staff, the close personal links between members of the relatively small elite, and the greater attractiveness of skilled jobs outside Transkei are exacerbating factors. At the lower (peasant) level, the apparent apathy can largely be explained as the result, inter alia, of a heavy dependency on migrant labour, restrictions on the normal processes of urbanisation, and a lack of any real official sympathy for and understanding of peasant motives and goals.

It is revealing—and a good indication of the usefulness of the discussions—that these two approaches came so strongly to the fore. Academics and grassroots community workers are naturally inclined to be more critical of existing structures and socio-economic and political relationships than senior civil servants and others who tend as a matter of course to identify with the structures of which they are a part. It is important, however, that the debate between the two sides continue, in order to promote the evolution of development strategies focused on both structural and personal constraints and opportunities.

In Search of a Strategy for Effective Development

Given that rural development was the central theme of the conference and that the empirical evidence on Transkeian agriculture indicates generally disappointing levels of performance, much soul-searching and debate was to be expected. The presence at the conference of senior officials of the Department of Agriculture added significance to the proceedings. Indeed, the Department was confronted by what may have appeared to be a coordinated attack on both its strategy for and practice of agricultural development over the past two decades. A barrage of criticism, both explicit and implied, was directed at the policy of village consolidation, betterment schemes, modern capital-intensive development projects, the shortage of extension officers, and the virtual absence of functioning cooperatives, as well as at the emphasis on maize at the expense of other crops. These and other criticisms were followed by proposals for a broadly conceived alternative strategy based on the need for "integrated rural development."

As could be expected, Government spokesmen felt compelled to counter this criticism of official agricultural policies. Mention was made of, inter alia, real successes in the fight against soil erosion, the viability of some of the larger capital-intensive projects, the inhibiting effects of a serious shortage of funds and trained staff, and widely differing regional performance leads. Moreover, those responsible for current policies were opposed to the seemingly radical nature of some of the counterproposals put forward in the name of "integrated rural development." On the basis of their experience they felt that at best policy changes had to be marginal or gradualist. However, since it became clearer in the course of the debate that a strategy of integrated rural development could itself only be implemented gradually and in carefully planned stages, the initial gap between the two sides narrowed. Even then, though, it was clear that the debate about new strategies and their implementation was only just beginning.

It seems clear that the potential contribution of academics to this debate will depend largely on their ability to understand and appreciate the practical and political problems inherent in strategy changes. Nevertheless, academics do have an important role to play, especially in refuting misconceptions about rural people and their way of life. The people living in Transkei's rural areas do not live in a separate, remote subsistence sector of the economy. They are on the contrary inextricably involved in the market economy and have cash and other needs similar to those of the urban population. Furthermore, while tribal people are influenced by tribal norms and "the traditional way of life," the economic decisions they take are generally rational and appropriate in terms of their circumstances and the options available to them.

If rural development is to be stimulated, it will be necessary to adjust priorities in government staffing, funding, and in the actual implementation of policy. To succeed in this, far more in-depth investigation of the rural environment and its dynamics will be necessary.

The Way Ahead

At the outset [of] the concluding workshop session, Prof. Thomas [indicated that the] Institute desired to play a catalytic role in exploring the merits of alternative strategies and in the investigation of specific policies or projects, and was willing to be of assistance as regards the technical aspects of research and planning. In addition, the Institute would place strong emphasis on training programmes complementary to those offered by the University, the Public Service Commission, and other bodies. He also saw a role for the Institute in focussing attention on issues and problems that might not always get sufficient attention. He cited as an example the migrant labour system, which probably was the single most important factor determining progress as regards both rural and urban development in Transkei.

A further task of the Institute and one endorsed by most delegates would be the collection and dissemination of relevant statistics and the undertaking of basic empirical research.

In several of the discussions consideration was given to matters related to the forthcoming Five-Year Plan. Several participants warned against the dangers of attaching inflated expectations to any one published document. Of greater significance than the initial document would be the establishment of a sound planning and plan consultation process, so that annual adjustments to this and future five-year plans would become an effective and appropriate instrument for the development of Transkei.

HONORS COURSE IN DEVELOPMENT PLANNING

[In 1981 the Institute for Management and Development Studies of the University of Transkei announced a new honors course in Development Planning. It exemplifies curricular innovation oriented toward African priorities.]

The one-year B Admin. (Hons) course in Development Planning is intended for graduates who are interested in the achievement of development in Southern Africa. The course is designed specifically to meet the needs of the public sector and is open to persons from a wide range of backgrounds who are presently employed, or who seek careers, in the public sector. As such it aims to meet the training needs for interdisciplinary development planning as well as the implementation of development projects.

Objectives

Development planning is concerned with people, their activities, the land, and the manner in which it is used. The task of development planning is to transform the available resources to meet people's needs as and where they occur.

A course in Development Planning must necessarily be comprehensive. It has to take into account simultaneously the economic, social, organisational, and physical aspects of development; and the coordination of national policies with local needs.

Content

The course includes the following prescribed modules:

- ☐ Third World Development
- ☐ Administrative and Personnel Issues
- ☐ Accounting for Development Management
- ☐ Development Strategies
- ☐ Aspects of Urban and Regional Planning

☐ Project and Programme Analysis
☐ Statistics and Research Methods

Specialised optional modules include:

☐ Agriculture and Rural Development
☐ Industrial and Commercial Development
☐ Planning for the Social Sector (including health and housing)
☐ Planning Educational Development

The course will involve lectures, seminars, and tutorials as well as practical field projects. Each module seeks to

☐ identify the main development issues;
☐ develop methods of analysis and problem solving;
☐ explore relevant planning policies;
☐ examine problems of policy implementation;
☐ develop an understanding of the context in which planners and policy makers will operate.

The emphasis of the course is on action-oriented approaches, coordinated decision-making, and the design of appropriate measures of intervention. Its focus is on the developing areas of Southern Africa.

Admission Requirements and Fees

The course is open to candidates who possess a good first degree in a wide range of disciplines including planning, commerce, education, engineering, agriculture, economics, geography, government, and social administration, or related fields. As a rule only persons with at least two years working experience will be admitted. Enrollment will be limited to about 12 per year.

The Honours course, introduced in 1982, is only offered on a full-time basis. Graduates of this course may be permitted to continue to a Masters programme in Development Planning.

The composite course fees including registration and study fees will be R500 in 1982. A few bursaries are available to cover part of the expenses.

The University of Bophuthatswana: An Africa-Oriented Open University (1980)

*The extent to which the University of Bophuthatswana (UNIBO) aspires to establish an exemplary model for higher education in South Africa becomes quickly evident from a reading of the following statement,*University of Bophuthatswana: Its Aims, Goals, and Structure *(Mafeking: UNIBO, 1980). Its establishment of four- rather than three-year degrees and its award of a two-year diploma are illustrative of its adaptation to community needs.*

The University and the Political Context

Although the Republic of Bophuthatswana was awarded independence by the Republic of South Africa under its policy of separate development, these circumstances do not imply that the new state in any way subscribes or adheres to that policy. With [independence,] Bophuthatswana turned its back irrevocably on the apartheid system and committed itself to the challenging priority of building a model of nondiscrimination that would act as catalyst in the whole Southern African Region. . . .

In [the eyes of its President], independence is therefore an interim phase in the evolution of a new dispensation in Southern Africa, acceptable to *all* people of the subcontinent and resting on the twin pillars of a closely knit Economic Community of Southern Africa ([modeled on] the European Common Market) and a con-federal tie-up between the subcontinent's political entities, founded on common allegiance to a Bill of Rights.

By accepting independence the government of Bophuthatswana gained the opportunity of making decisions guided by the interests of its people and their social, cultural, and economic development. The fact that Bophuthatswana has to develop its own economic structure on the periphery of the strong South African economy has presented the Government with a set of peculiar but challenging opportunities as well as problems.

In the field of education, independence has meant the possibility of evolving a system more in tune with the needs of the community than could be achieved under South African policy. This freedom to innovate in educational structures and curricula will facilitate the emergence of a university giving priority to the interests of its immediate constituency and having relevance to its developmental problems and opportunities.

Like other universities on the subcontinent, the University of Bophuthatswana is subsidised by the government, but in terms of its charter it will remain essentially autonomous. It is controlled by a Council made up of professional people and academics, both Black and White, representing a wide spectrum of professional skills and interests. They have been appointed in terms of an Act of the National Assembly which establishes the University as an autonomous body. The only criterion used in the appointment of these people has been their commitment to education and development in Bophuthatswana. The Council appoints all staff [i.e., faculty] and in their teaching, research, and way of life they will be encouraged to contribute to development of the theoretical framework and the practical projects necessary for the emergence of a "post-separate development" dispensation in Southern Africa. The University is therefore a nonracial institution with full academic freedom to determine whom it will appoint, whom it will enroll as a student, and what it will teach.

A decision to work in the University of Bophuthatswana therefore does not in any way mean support for separate development. On the contrary, it means dedication to work for the establishment of a nonracial, nondiscriminatory society. It is therefore hoped that academics from elsewhere in Africa as well as from the world at large will join those from Southern Africa in helping to build a uniquely innovative institution in a subcontinent in urgent need of the kind of creative initiative exemplified by the founding of the University of Bophuthatswana. It is equally hoped that students from elsewhere in Africa as well as from the world at large will join those from Bophuthatswana at the University to participate in the exciting venture of seeking ways and means of establishing an alternative society where cultural and social differences are not a source of estrangement and conflict, but rather a source of mutual enrichment and unity. . . .

[History and Aims]

THE UNIVERSITY AND THE PEOPLE

The University of Bophuthatswana was born not in the minds of educational planners, but in the hearts of the people. During the late 1960s and early part of the 1970s a spontaneous movement took place among the people of Bophuthatswana which led, in spite of their dire economic situation, to them raising more than one hundred thousand Rand as their contribution to the establishment of an [indigenous] university for Bophuthatswana. However, they had to wait for political independence before this wish could become reality.

THE REPORT OF THE NATIONAL EDUCATION COMMISSION 1978

In August 1978 the National Education Commission of the Republic of Bophuthatswana, under the chairmanship of Prof E. P. Lekhela, presented its report to the government. Chapter 23 of the report deals with the University, its nature, "where it should be sited, what its priorities should be in relation to the needs of the country and of what kind of men [are] to be chosen to lead it." Among the general considerations as to the nature of the University put forward by the Commission [and] endorsed by the government in October 1978 were the following:

☐ It is a basic premise of your Commission that the University should be part of the community, would be sensitive to its needs and serve them.

☐ Culturally the University must not only fulfil the function of every university but . . . [also] reflect the culture of the Batswana people and contribute to its development in a changing society.

☐ The University of Bophuthatswana, in addition to the normal tasks of a university—to teach, to foster research, and to disseminate knowledge—should bear in mind its special functions in a developing country. The specific needs of Bophuthatswana, academic, cultural, as well as technical, should be catered for. University graduates should not consider themselves merely as academics, but as men and women who can dedicate their minds, hearts, and hands to the development of their country. Finally, the University must pursue the goals of social and individual excellence—physical, mental, and spiritual—so that the student will be committed to the furtherance of human dignity and worth, as well as social and economic development. There should be close cooperation between the University and the State so that the interests of the country are served, its problems investigated, and a response made to its deepest needs.

☐ In the ethos of the University emphasis [should] be placed on the development of the community and not solely on the individual development of the student.

☐ Academic courses [should focus] initially on [vital needs of] economic and social development, and make the maximum use of the country's human potential. . . .

☐ The University must form an umbrella body linking together all forms of tertiary education into one integrated system with possibilities of interchangeability of facilities and mobility of students from one type of tertiary education to another.

THE UNIVERSITY OF BOPHUTHATSWANA ACT, 1978

Following on the passing of the University of Bophuthatswana Act (No. 10 of 1978) the Council of the University was appointed by the President in Executive Council and held its first formal meeting on 28 September 1978. Members of the Council represent a wide cross section of academic, educational, church, and business interests in Southern Africa.

BROAD UNIVERSITY POLICY

The Council found itself in unanimous agreement with the broad principles put forward by the National Education Commission as briefly indicated earlier. In the further elucidation of these, the Council placed on record the following [policies]:

□ While instituted primarily to serve the needs of Bophuthatswana and its people, the University [is] envisaged [as] an open institution. It will admit any student who satisfies the requirements laid down for admission and for whom accommodation and courses are available. The ideal of the Council is an open university in an open society.

□ In the appointment of staff, positive efforts will be made to recruit and develop academics and administrators who are citizens of Bophuthatswana. However, it will clearly also be necessary to appoint expatriate staff for some time to come. It is hoped that other universities will find it possible to support the new University by sending members of staff for varying periods, at the same time protecting their status in their own university. There will also be a place for some academics from other countries, who could share in contributing to the University that universality which, alongside its character as an African university, should be one of its hallmarks. In seeking innovative and pioneering staff the Council will consider not only the academic qualifications and experience of applicants but also the personal qualities and understanding that would equip them for this task.

□ It is of vital importance for any new university seeking recognition by the international academic community that from the beginning it establish and thereafter maintain acceptable academic standards.

In a policy document dated 29 April 1979 the Council also set out among others the following guidelines for the University:

□ The University is to comprise a federation of colleges, with University headquarters and the central academic college situated at the capital of the country, Mmabatho. Other constituents of the University, some of which will be situated elsewhere in Bophuthatswana, will be: a college or colleges for advanced technical and commercial education; a college for agriculture (the nucleus for this already exists at Taung); a number of colleges of education.

□ On the Mmabatho campus priority is given to the setting up of programmes in teacher training, law, commerce, and administration. By making these courses available to teachers and civil servants it is hoped that the University will have an immediate impact on the efficiency and capability of the governmental and educational services.

□ As a necessary support to these professional programmes a strong core of basic academic courses will also be introduced immediately, from [which] will develop, as the need arises, the various academic directions that are the proper concern of any university.

□ In seeking to make its most effective contribution to the development of the human potential of Bophuthatswana, the University will of necessity have to turn its attention to two major areas of concern:

(a) The large number of mature students at the tertiary level who may not be in possession of formal qualifications for entry into university.

(b) The grave shortage of graduate teachers in the secondary school system, which has resulted in the pupils from these schools, even [those with] matriculation certificates, being inadequately prepared for university studies.

☐ Degree, diploma, and certificate courses will offer [a variety of] options to the student. The University [will] provide orientation programmes, courses to bridge the gap between school and university, and special programmes in study skills, English, and communication. Because of the [lack of] sufficient students with adequate standards in mathematics and the sciences, the University may have to initiate a "junior college" to provide entrants with this competency.

☐ Particularly in the early years, serious consideration will have to be given to the needs of the mature, part-time student. This will necessitate greater flexibility in the structuring of curricula to allow of, for example, a modular system of building up credits towards the completion of qualifications.

☐ From the beginning high priority will be given to the development of an effective system [of] admissions, to develop the natural abilities of students, reduce the damaging effects of failure, and to safeguard academic and professional standards.

☐ In the early years of the University there inevitably will be some important fields of study in which it will be unable to offer [courses]. Students in these fields will have to attend other institutions. But it is important for the human resources [of] Bophuthatswana that these students be linked in some way with the University of Bophuthatswana. This could be done if government bursaries were channeled through the University, by the provision of courses preparing students for entry to other universities, and by constant monitoring of their progress by arrangement with the university they are attending.

University Structure and Function

Although the university is always [evolving], it has to take on a specific form and function at a specific time and place, stemming from the needs and aspirations of the society in which it finds itself.

INNOVATION

Both the National Education Commission [and] His Excellency the President [in his] inaugural address to the Council stressed that the University should not necessarily follow the pattern of the classical Western university, but should seek to establish a structure that would be relevant to the needs of the country. The University thus has a mandate to innovate. This mandate places a great responsibility on the planners as well as on the selectors of staff, as overhasty appointments could lead to the innovative dimension being replaced by the well-known structure and functions of the traditional university. Innovation is not a once-only event, but should be built into the structure [of the University] so that the whole system will continuously reassess itself. . . .

[TEACHING VERSUS RESEARCH]

The University will concentrate at first on being primarily an undergraduate teaching institution. No university system can be entirely educationally orientated, but the main emphasis in the University will be the educational impact on the student and the community. The total development of the student will not be left to chance, but will [be] specifically planned and monitored. The goal will be to produce a person who is competent to function within a modern, increasingly technologically orientated society and able as well as willing to contribute to the development of this society.

Research will be an integral part of the whole University system, including the Colleges. The curricula must be designed so as to develop in the student an approach to *problem-solving* which takes into consideration the impact of his research, as well as the influence of his proposals and solutions on the whole system within which he operates. Research will therefore not be an individual enterprise based on the interest of the researcher, but will be directed towards the developmental needs of the subject, the institution, the student, and the country, with priority given to research into local problems that will contribute to the amelioration of the life of the ordinary man.

This means that the University will take into consideration for promotion and other purposes teaching ability and interest [and] community service. The University will thus implement a more flexible system of reward than the one in common use in universities.

Cultural Relevance and Modernisation

The University functions within a specific culture (which is undergoing rapid change) and must take cognisance of the cultural background of students and the problems and opportunities that that background presents. The University will of necessity also influence that culture and it should continuously be analysing the long-term effects of its educational system upon it.

Professor N. O. P. Setidisho, Rector of the University College of Botswana, at a graduation address in 1976 spoke of the importance of relevance in the teaching and research of the new university.

> University teaching must [foster] the acquisition of certain psychological, social, and cultural attitudes implicit in development in the individual, his family, the community around him, and the nation as a whole: rational thought, organisation, enterprise, the habit of saving, technical and economic inventiveness, aesthetic taste, cooperation, social and civic awareness, active participation in political life, and a deep belief in progress; these qualities in turn having an influence on health, emotional stability, family life, national unity and identity, international understanding, and the economic development of the country.

SUPPORT SYSTEMS

The University must also take note of the special problems experienced by students coming from strongly traditional backgrounds who now face acute stresses and pressures of cultural modernisation. Special support systems will be necessary to assist them through this transition. *Every staff member* at the University must be prepared to be counsellor as well as guidance officer and teacher and to work in close cooperation with the counselling and career guidance services.

AVAILABILITY OF STAFF

The transfer of the ethos of a specific discipline or vocation takes place to some extent by the student modelling [himself] on his teacher. Such transfer takes place only in a relationship of trust and respect that can be described as a "pastoral care" relationship. *Availability* and *visibility* of the teacher with regard to the student will therefore be built into the system.

STUDENT DEVELOPMENT

Although it will be an open university accepting any student qualifying for admission, the majority of students will come from a background that can be described as non-technological and with an affiliative rather than an achievement-based motivational pattern. This sociocultural background tends to limit the capacity of students to function effectively and to compete both in the University and in the modern technologically orientated world in which they have to survive. Apart from vocational and general formative education and training, the University will [therefore] have to accept responsibility for training students in basic educational, communicative, and study skills. This is however not enough. It will also be necessary to train students of all levels within the University towards an achievement-orientated motivational pattern to enable them to cope with the demands placed on people in positions [of responsibility and authority], thus enabling them to contribute to the socioeconomic development of the country.

Professional competence and excellence can however never be the sole end-point of any educational system, [as] this may lead to the graduate exploiting his employer, his profession, and the community to serve only himself. Professional competence must always be tempered by responsibility towards the profession and the community. In any country, compassion and concern for his fellowmen must be developed in every student who has the privilege of tertiary education and training. If this is not done an educated elite is produced who develop only themselves and who have no developmental impact on their fellowmen or on the various systems of the country.

Furthermore, professional competence as one of the end criteria should not be interpreted to mean that the system [should] produce "good" employees, passively subject to the employer or the work situation. The aim will be to develop autonomous individuals with competence, drive, and a work ethic that relates them to society and [enables them] to innovate in whatever situation they find themselves. This should produce an *entrepreneurial spirit* in the country—individuals that can accept responsibility to their society. It is not necessary that an entrepreneurial spirit should constrain or even clash with a student's feelings of concern and compassion.

This concern of the University to assist the student in the process of cultural transition or cultural modernisation implies a certain amount of involvement in the *pre-tertiary* educational field. Professional and vocational education and training from the standard eight level for selected students enables the basis for cultural transition to be laid at a receptive age and, where necessary, enables the formal thought-patterns for mathematics and the natural sciences to be laid. This will not only improve the tertiary achievement of the student but will also assist him in the cultural transition from a non-technical culture.

WORK EXPERIENCE AS PART OF THE EDUCATION PROGRAMME

The Israeli experience has shown that in educational systems spanning disparate cultures, the internalisation of technological and academic concepts is particularly facilitated by repeated experience of actual work situations. This experience and its interaction with the academic programme tend to eliminate the knowledge and values which are dysfunctional to professional situations and thereby increase the efficiency of the whole training programme and the competence of its products. At the same time students will find their academic courses much more relevant and rewarding. If the student is furthermore remunerated to some extent for his labour one can expect a considerably improved morale and motivation to progress. This inclusion of practical work experience in the University curriculum reemphasises close cooperation of the University and the private and public sector. It follows logically that work situations will be closely related to academic curricula and contribute to the final evaluation of the student.

Professional and Vocational Emphasis

In order to maximise its effect on the developmental needs of the student and the country, and in order to establish a specific and defined goal for the educational process, the University will have a strong professional emphasis—using the word *professional* here in its widest possible sense. This means that the curricula will be so designed that the end product on every level within the system will be professionally competent. This means again that curricula and educational methods must be designed with requirements of the future work situation or vocational field in mind.

The University system will therefore, initially at least, concentrate on professional education and training in order to satisfy the most urgent manpower needs of Bophuthatswana as a developing country as well as the need of the student to be able to compete in an economic system that in many ways may be culturally foreign to him.

In order to ensure an economic growth rate that will enable all the peoples of Southern Africa to enjoy an acceptable standard of living, it is primarily necessary for the educational system to produce two categories of persons—technically skilled persons to develop the technical infrastructure, and managers. [These individuals must be able to] operate autonomously as *entrepreneurs* in a technological system while maintaining a relationship of *care and compassion* towards society.

The University must have built into its framework the ethic of contribution to the development of the community in which it stands. This contribution should not only be indirect through the quality and skill of its students, but also direct by the inclusion of community service and development work in University programmes. The student should experience from the very beginning an immediate responsibility to society and he should see this responsibility in action in the work and lives of his teachers. *Every subject should provide a service outside the school or college, in the community.*

An important aspect of this community responsibility lies in not allowing separation to develop between the University and the community. The University must not be allowed to [become] an isolated community. Recreational, cultural, and even teaching facilities will be open to the community. Student accommodation, especially for senior students, will be in the community.

Putting a student in a position to experience concretely the problems of development and to contribute to their solution follows logically from a combination of the University's development orientation and its vocational emphasis. In such a study-service scheme students *will be able to take an active part* in development programmes. Whether he participates as a teacher, health officer, etc., [a student] will experience very concretely the meaning of his country's problems [in] his Development Studies course. In this way he repays some of his debt to the country for his education and narrows the rural-urban and elite-mass communication gaps so damaging to a growing democracy. By drawing community members into the planning, organisation, and evaluation of student work, study-service schemes [disseminate] the meaning of both the University as an institution and the imperatives of development.

The University System and Tertiary Education

According to the Report of the Lekhela Commission all tertiary education in Bophuthatswana should be taken up in the university. To express this structurally, it means that the University must in fact consist of a University system consisting of a central campus as well as several colleges spread across the country. This enables students to be channelled in this system according to ability, aptitude and the needs of the country.

[To prepare students for the colleges] the University may have to become involved in pre-tertiary professional training and education.

A direct contribution will be made to the training of those professional and vocational categories for which there is a tremendous need at present (clerks, teachers, technicians, nurses, and skilled workers).

[These programs] will in turn act as a source of selected students for tertiary education and training within the University system in various vocational and professional fields, [including] technical and vocational teaching. [With the availability of teachers and the establishment of] professional schools, the University [will be able] to shed its pre-tertiary commitment in due course.

Professional Emphasis and University Structure

It has been explained that the University would, for the first phase in its development, concentrate on being an undergraduate teaching institution with a strong emphasis on professional and vocational education and training, giving special attention to equipping the students to function effectively in the modern technological environment.

This professional emphasis finds structural expression in the fact that the system will consist of a series of professional colleges as well as in the fact that the central campus at Mmabatho will not consist of the traditional faculties, but will consist of Professional Schools, e.g., School of Education, School of Law.

This emphasis has also influenced the course structure. All degrees will as far as possible be four-year degrees and will consist of two parts of two years each. At the end of the first phase of two years the students will obtain a diploma. Only selected students will be allowed to proceed to the degree programme.

The reason for instituting the initial diploma programme is that it provides a selection point at which students who clearly will not succeed in the degree programme can either terminate their studies with a professional qualification or go on to a Higher Diploma. This Higher Diploma will however be so designed as to offer an attractive primary option for many students. By this method it is hoped to minimise the number of students who drop out of University programmes without obtaining a qualification and who consequently receive no recognition from employers for the time spent at University.

Many of our students [cannot meet] the requirements of the Joint Matriculation Board, due to present educational circumstances beyond control. Potentially, however, they are "degree-standard" candidates. In order to assist them to obtain an academic qualification it is being recommended that an Advanced Diploma be instituted, of which the curriculum, syllabi, and standards required will correspond exactly with those of the degree programme.

This Advanced Programme will permit students to enter postgraduate studies, both here at UNIBO and at other universities in the subcontinent that allow entry on the basis of degree-equivalent qualifications. The Higher Diploma will allow for further study opportunities for those students who do not qualify for the degree or advanced diploma programmes, but will also be a primary option for many students.

The four-year degree is an integrated degree course replacing in many instances the three-year degree followed by the one-year professional diploma. In this integrated structure, completion of the first diploma however does not guarantee admission to the degree course. The actual performance of the student will be taken into consideration in deciding upon his admission to either the second phase of the degree or the Higher Diploma. The first diploma will already be a definite, recognised professional qualification which will enable the student to enter the labour market. A person attending a corresponding professional college will receive a diploma which will give access to selected students to the second part of the degree course at the central campus.

Compulsory Subjects

□ Communication and Study Skills: The aim of the course is to teach the students the skills of communicating in a second language. This is necessary as the medium of instruction in the school system and at the University is English. Certain study skills will also be included in the course.

☐ Development Studies: The University's basic educational policy requires that the students in all curricula be led to understand the factors and processes of development, particularly in relation to Southern Africa in general and Bophuthatswana in particular. This necessitates an inter-disciplinary course in Development Studies in the curriculum. Such a course will draw on the insights of history, geography, sociology and economics, and can include the study of concrete development projects in process or planned in Bophuthatswana.

☐ Quantitative Methods: This course in basic numeracy will be aimed at developing the quantitative skills necessary for University study as well as to equip the student to interpret and use the quantitative data on which effective functioning in modern society is based.

The Technikon Approach to Higher Education (1980)

The Peninsula Technikon's brochure sets forth the concept and scope of its educational program and development plans.

The Technikon Approach

The stream of tertiary education in South Africa has taken a new and interesting turn in the approach to practical education. This new form of advanced education is different from anything that has existed in South Africa before. When compared to universities the following emerge:

☐ Universities are mainly responsible for providing the theoretical academic stream of education.

☐ Technikons are mainly providing practically oriented education.

The creative thinker must be fostered by the universities in the climate of intellectual, academic, and conceptual thinking.

The skilled practical doer will be the product of the Technikon.

The enormous need for technological knowledge with which South Africa and the rest of the world have been confronted and the giant technological strides taken by man, causing an unprecedented need for manpower, demand dynamic development of practically oriented knowledge besides the traditional theoretical academic studies.

Technikons have a duty towards commerce and industry. Employers are strongly pushing for [graduates of] tertiary institutions who would be trained not only in the most modern of techniques but who would immediately be productive on entering the highly competitive arena of industry and commerce.

Technikons and employers therefore collaborate by means of advisory committees consisting of lecturers and experts from industry and commerce. This collaboration is a frutiful one, for not only are syllabuses revised and planned by these committees, but new courses are piloted as well.

Commerce sets the highest standards: it requires business people with skill and judgement, people who have realised their full potential. The prime objective of the Peninsula Technikon is to produce such men and women.

The Hierarchy of Qualifications

A radical change has taken place within the hierarchy of qualifications that can be obtained at Technikons. This is the result of

☐ the tremendous increase in knowledge in virtually all fields;
☐ the rapid development in almost every type of profession;
☐ practice-oriented professional training at Technikons;
☐ the accompanying modification of existing knowledge;
☐ the aim of the Technikons to train students in such a way that they are able to be productive in their particular fields within the shortest possible time;
☐ the shortage of skilled manpower in South Africa.

Owing to this evolution, new courses and syllabuses have been devised and are offered at all Technikons. The course for a first qualification is compiled with a view to the immediate and short-term requirements of the profession concerned. As this profession starts making greater demands and adding more responsibilities, the initial training can be followed by more advanced study, leading to a further qualification.

Applied and developmental research, emphasising the fact that the end result should have immediate practical value, forms an integral part of these courses and this research becomes progressively more important as the student advances to higher qualifications. At the fifth- and sixth-year level students are required to do applied and/or developmental research to qualify as specialists in their field.

Training Systems

The Technikon provides practical training courses which complement the traditional academic courses offered at universities. The Technikon student is thus introduced to the practical work situation at a very early stage in his training. The system which progressively integrates academic study with practical training is known as Cooperative Training.

Cooperative Training aims at combining academic and professional training with practical training to develop the maximum potential of the students.

The following options are available:

□ *Full-time courses.* Full-time students attend classes at the Technikon for a minimum period of a year. During this period they also do practical work in the workshop and laboratories.

□ *Part-time courses.* Individuals in full-time employment may improve their qualifications by attending the various evening classes conducted by the Technikon.

□ *Sandwich courses.* Students study full-time at the Technikon for part of the year and receive on-the-job training at their places of employment for the rest of the year. Courses of this nature are primarily followed by students training to become technicians and technologists. Normally prospective candidates have to be employed before they can embark on their training, though this is not a requirement. Course programmes can also be planned to allow students to attend classes for either one or two days per week or for half days.

[Peninsula students receive technical training in a wide array of subjects in schools of Commerce and Management, Teacher Training, Engineering and Building, and Applied Sciences. As part of the expansion of Technikon education throughout South Africa, Peninsula's enrollment is projected to reach 10,000 by the year 2000.]

DOCUMENT XVII:

Consulting Banned Books (1981)

*Students wishing access to banned or restricted books and re-
search material must fill in request forms countersigned by an
instructor. Many hesitate about leaving such a trail of potential
interest to the security police. The following application forms
for consulting (1) "prohibited" and (2) "undesirable" publications are used at the UNISA library, where availability is
more likely and use less attention provoking than at black universities. (Despite "independence," the University of Transkei's
library remains constrained by the same lists of prohibited and
restricted publications as libraries of other South African
institutions.)*

SANLAM LIBRARY, UNIVERSITY OF SOUTH AFRICA

1. *Application for the use of a publication which has been prohibited by the Department of Justice*

   I hereby declare that I (name in block letters) ....
   ....

   ☐ am a lecturer at UNISA, attached to the Department of ...
   ....

   ☐ am a postgraduate student at Unisa, registered for the course ....,
   and that I require the undermentioned publication, which has been prohibited by the Department of Justice, for *bona fide* research purposes for use in the Library only.

   Author: ....
   Title: ....
   ....

   Class. no. .... Accession no. ....

   Signature .... Date ....
   Student no. .... Identity no. ....

2. *Approval of the application by the Director of Library Services*
   Signature .... Date ....

3. *Record of use*
   Made available on ....
   Signature...

N.B. 1. The Unisa Library has an open exemption from the Department of Justice to make available publications prohibited by that department. The exemption is subject to the condition "that only lecturers and students who are engaged in *bona fide* postgraduate study be permitted to make use of the publications under the control and supervision of the University, and that such publications be housed in a safe place and that a register of use be maintained."

2. Your attention is drawn to the fact that these publications may not be quoted from without the permission of the Minister of Justice.

SANLAM LIBRARY, UNIVERSITY OF SOUTH AFRICA

1. *Application for the use of a publication which has been declared undesirable.*
I hereby declare that I (name in block letters) ....
....

☐ am a lecturer at UNISA, attached to the Department of ....
....

☐ am an undergraduate/postgraduate (delete what is not applicable) student at UNISA, registered for the course ....
....

and that I require the undermentioned publication, which appears on the official list of undesirable publications, for research purposes:
Author ....
Title ....
Class.no. .... Accession no. ....

☐ I request that the publication be made available to me for use in the Library only.
☐ I request that the publication be issued to me for use at home (N.B. only lecturers and postgraduate students). I undertake:
– to keep the publication under lock and key when it is not actually being used by me;
– not to make any reproductions or copies of the publication except for *bona fide* study, teaching, research, or reference purposes.
☐ I request that a photocopy of the publication be furnished to me (p. ...... to p. ......). I undertake to make no further reproductions or copies thereof.

Registration no. .... Identity no. ....
Date .... Signature ....

2. *Approval of the application by the Director of Library Services*
☐ For use in the Library only. Signature ....
☐ For home use. Signature ....
☐ For provision of photocopies. Signature ....

3. *Approval of the application by the Head of the Teaching Department*
For home use. Signature ....

4. *Record of use*
☐ Use in library. Date ....
☐ Issued on .... Returned on ....
☐ Photocopies provided, p. ...... to p. ......
Signature ....

Conditions for making undesirable publications available

1. The publication may only be consulted for *bona fide* study, teaching, research or reference purposes, certified as such after proper identification by the Director of Library Services and, in doubtful cases, in consultation with the head of the department to which the student is attached.

2. Undergraduate students may only consult the publication in the Library under supervision.

3. With the approval of both the Director of Library Services and the relevant teaching department, publications may be issued to lecturers and postgraduate students for home use on the following conditions:
   – that the publication be kept under lock and key when it is not actually in use by him.
   – that copies of the publication not be made for any reason other than *bona fide* study, teaching, research, or reference purposes.

4. Photocopies may only be provided after approval by the Director of Library Services, and then only in respect of a publication for which consultation has already been certified as set out in par. 1. The provision of photocopies is subject to the condition that no further copy thereof will be made by the person to whom the photocopies are supplied.

5. Consultation of the publications (use in the library, issue for home use or provision of photocopies) must be recorded in a register. The name of the publication, the name and identity number of the person consulting it, as well as the date of consultation, must be entered in the register.

U.S. Responses to the Educational Needs of Black South Africans:

An Address by Assistant Secretary of State for African Affairs Chester A. Crocker (1981)

> *The following is the abridged text of Dr. Crocker's remarks to a colloquium on "Furthering Higher Education of Black South Africans: How Can the United States Best Help?" convened by the African Studies Program of Georgetown University's Center for Strategic and International Studies on December 17-18, 1981.*

Throughout South Africa's history education has played a central role in defining social goals and as an engine for social change. The significance of education to the Afrikaners was underscored in the National Party's 1948 Manifesto for Christian National Education which stated that "Native education should be based on the principles of trusteeship, non-equality, and segregation; its aims should be to inculcate the white man's way of life, especially that of the Boer nation, which is the senior trustee." In 1981, education remains a key engine of social change in South Africa, with some important differences. The Report of the Human Sciences Research Council (HSRC) Investigation into Education stands in stark contrast to the 1948 National Party manifesto. The HSRC, as its first principle for the Provision of Education in the Republic of South Africa, asserts that "Equal opportunities in education, for every inhabitant, irrespective of race, color, creed, or sex, shall be the purposeful endeavor of the State."

The HSRC report is a signal of the process of change that is underway in South Africa. But, as in the areas of economic and political change, the extent of social change and therefore the true nature of South Africa's education reform remain undefined.

Formal changes in the constitutional structure providing for power sharing have not yet taken place. Nevertheless, for the first time the Government has created a multiracial, consultative body in the President's Council (which includes "coloreds" and Asians, but not Africans). The task of this body is to make recommendations to the Government for legislative or other action concerning a new constitutional framework for South Africa. We fully recognize the limited nature of the representation on the President's Council—the deliberate exclusion of Africans and the apparent failure of the Government to act on some of the Council's initial recommendations. A final determination on the President's Council may be possible after the submission of its recommendations. In the interim, it is important to note that the President's Council represents a partly inclusive multiracial deliberative body at the national political level.

There have also been other developments which, although not essentially political, are particularly important for the future of South Africa's blacks. They indicate that South Africa is beginning to think in terms of one unitary economy encompassing all its people, rather than eleven separate ones. We have seen the South African Government moving to

□ co-opt the private sector through the forging of an informal political, military, and business elite as an ally in the reform effort;

□ emphasize regional development based more on economic growth than on ideological consideration as in the past. The new strategy embodies both development corridors (deconcentration) and regional growth poles (decentralization);

□ establish a workable labor conciliation mechanism;

□ accept in practice, if not in principle, the permanence of some urban blacks through the creation of a ninety-nine-year leasehold program and demonstrate more responsiveness to their economic needs and aspirations. In this regard, the South African Government recently authorized, for the first time, private real estate development in the urban black townships, thereby abandoning the Government's monopoly on township housing and eliminating a major obstacle to alleviating the chronic black housing shortage.

Although all developments in the implementation of the limited reform program outlined above have not been clearly positive, there are some indicators of forward movement. These indicators include the following:

□ As a result of black wage gains in manufacturing and mining, the black share of national income has risen appreciably since 1970. The ratio of white wages to African wages in manufacturing dropped from 5.8 to 1 in 1970 to 4.3 to 1 in 1979. In mining, it dropped from 19.8 to 1 to 6.6 to 1 over the same period. Some redistribution of wealth from whites to blacks as a group has probably taken place.

□ Some petty apartheid has been eliminated, as well as certain restrictions on black business and housing. [But] many of these changes in petty apartheid have been made by creating special legal exemptions to apartheid laws, the basic structure of which remains intact.

□ Most significant with respect to the basic economic structure, black unions have won recognition and black apprentice training has been accelerated.

□ The Government has moved to deracialize sports by eliminating all Government laws and regulations in this area, permitting sports bodies and athletes to compete on the basis of personal choice.

□ Within the context of the structure of separate education in South Africa the South African Government appears to be taking a first step toward greater equality in education. This commitment has largely gone unnoticed by world public opinion which remains focused on the continued separation within the educational system.

Starting this year, free compulsory education through the seventh grade is being phased in for black Africans in selected areas. However, this program is not expected to be in place nationwide until 1992. Black enrollment at "white" universities in [courses] not [offered at] segregated black schools has grown substantially. Spending on black education has increased. . . .

The South African Government in its response to the Human Sciences Research Council has emphasized its continuing commitment to separate education. What is changing from previous Government policy, therefore, is not the separateness of education, a manifestation of apartheid, but its inherent inequality. Even with this change in policy the extent of that inequality is of such a magnitude as to call into question the South African Government's ability to redress the imbalance. We are, therefore, dealing with two parallel and inseparable issues; the system which has produced these inequities and the commitment and will to redress them.

In the context of changes in South African Government perceptions of its educational goals, an opportunity exists for the United States and other like-minded nations to play a helpful role in meeting the educational needs of disadvantaged black South Africans. The Government's continued commitment to separate education, however, raises questions about the nature and extent of United States involvement with education in South Africa. To the extent that separation in education continues to be a keystone of South Africa's apartheid policy, United States involvement in South African education must be clearly distinguished from a separate-but-equal policy we ourselves have rejected as unacceptable.

However, in recognition of the process of change that is now underway in South Africa and to the extent that education is a key to that change, the United States would be remiss in not participating in addressing the educational needs of those black South Africans who are the recipients of separate and unequal education.

Three markers must be observed in attempting to design a U.S. response to the educational needs of black South Africans. First, any approach which is interventionist in nature will be opposed by the South African Government as it would by any sovereign government. Second, any approach which calls on the United States to play the role that is properly that of the South African Government will be opposed by that portion of the population it is intended to benefit. Third, our approach should be formulated in consultation with South Africans of all groups, including, particularly, the black community. It should reflect their needs and priorities and not be dictated to them.

A programmatic approach based purely on scholarships for study abroad offers one method of addressing these needs and priorities. Such an approach, though, only partially addresses the various aspects of educational advancement for South Africa's black communities. It would not address the educational needs of those students who failed to make the grade as scholarship candidates. In effect, a purely scholarship program could be said to benefit the top achievers within apartheid education while writing off apartheid education's saddest victims.

The multiple dimensions of the South African educational equation are being considered by the Administration as we review the substance and possible structure of a broader U.S. response to the educational needs of black South Africans both in terms of the educational system and the need of students themselves. The policy review process takes into account the advantages of education in the U.S. as opposed to South Africa, of undergraduate versus postgraduate education, and of formal university education versus vocational training. It is also considering curriculum development, teacher training, bridging programs, technical skills training, management training, and educational [uses of] television.

As in our overall approach to relations with South Africa, our focus in the educational area is on the process of change that is underway. In the area of education as well as elsewhere, change in South Africa is primarily motivated by enlightened self-interest. Certainly it would be difficult to ascribe the change that is underway to the plethora of rhetorical exhortations, sanctions, and punitive measures which have been invoked against South Africa over the past two decades. More likely it is coming from the pressures and realities of South African society itself and the efforts of South Africans of all races who are convinced of the need for change.

If change is underway in South Africa, albeit slowly, the choice confronting South Africa between radical violent revolution and peaceful evolutionary change is becoming ever more starkly drawn. It is too simple a dichotomy, but in a sense the choice which confronts South Africa and those who would influence it lies in part between the battlefield and classroom. Certainly, failure in the latter will hasten violent confrontation on the former. Education is, therefore, central to peaceful evolutionary change; in that sense the classroom suggests itself as one very important key to our policy toward South Africa. We are dealing in this instance not with a rhetorical position, but rather with the requirements of a considered and sustained foreign policy initiative reflecting balanced U.S. interests and contributing to peaceful resolution of South Africa's unsettled political agenda.

We believe that education of black South Africans is an appropriate field for U.S. attention for three reasons: First, because we perceive that South Africans of all races welcome such cooperation; second, because such attention is change-oriented but not interventionist in the sensitive area of sovereign political and legal structures; and third, because we and others know education is a central variable in the process that will influence attitudes and opportunities in years ahead.

The question U.S. policy must therefore address is how we relate the classroom to our interests in peaceful evolutionary change. More precisely, our policy is aimed at developing a package of educational initiatives which will act to encourage a constructive process motivated by self-interest and not hindered by the continuing ideology of separateness on the one hand or the ideology of armed struggle as the only option, on the other. Our goal is to harness that self-interest [to the interest in peaceful change we all share].

We are moving toward such a peaceful [resolution of] the problems of southern Africa in Angola, Namibia, and South Africa. As an Administration we have eschewed rhetoric in favor of quiet diplomacy. In dealing directly with South Africa's apartheid policy it is incumbent upon us to do so in a sober and realistic fashion, laying aside domestic partisan political postures which have sometimes divided us in favor of the common goal which unites us.

Significant steps in the area of education have already been taken by foundations and firms in the private sector. The Institute of International Education's South Africa Education Program is significant among these efforts. Also noteworthy is the PACE commercial high school which offers yet another possible approach to the problem.

As a government the United States has also renewed its long-standing commitment to helping meet the educational needs of South African and Namibian refugee students. We are undertaking two programs in FY 82. First, the United States will initiate a new intake of 50 Namibian and South African refugee students this year under the Southern Africa Training Program. Through this program nearly 800 southern African students have been placed in university and other post-secondary training programs since 1976.

Second, the United States has contributed $1 million to the United Nations Education and Training Program for Southern Africa in FY 82. This program will also directly benefit Namibian and South African refugee students.

The refugee education programs add a valuable element to a mix of scholarships and in-country programs designed to further remedy the educational inequalities inherent in South Africa's apartheid policies.

In conclusion, let me reiterate the U.S. commitment to helping in meeting the educational needs of black South Africans and to underscore our view that education is a key to the process of social change in South Africa. The question is complex. There is no single or simple answer. Our approach as a government is, therefore, to be as responsive as possible to the multiple interests involved through a broad range of educational activities, all of which are linked by their orientation toward both educational equality and social change.

Index

Designer:	UC Press and Wilsted & Taylor
Compositor:	Wilsted & Taylor
Printer:	Vail-Ballou
Binder:	Vail-Ballou
Text:	10/13 Baskerville
Display:	Palatino